T0120643

The
Morning After

SURVIVING THE LOSS OF SOMEONE YOU LOVE

John M Samony Sr, CGSS

WESTBOW
PRESS®
A DIVISION OF THOMAS NELSON
& ZONDERVAN

Copyright © 2021 John M Samony Sr, CGSS.

All rights reserved. No part of this book may be used or reproduced by any means, graphic, electronic, or mechanical, including photocopying, recording, taping or by any information storage retrieval system without the written permission of the author except in the case of brief quotations embodied in critical articles and reviews.

This book is a work of non-fiction. Unless otherwise noted, the author and the publisher make no explicit guarantees as to the accuracy of the information contained in this book and in some cases, names of people and places have been altered to protect their privacy.

WestBow Press books may be ordered through booksellers or by contacting:

WestBow Press
A Division of Thomas Nelson & Zondervan
1663 Liberty Drive
Bloomington, IN 47403
www.westbowpress.com
844-714-3454

Because of the dynamic nature of the Internet, any web addresses or links contained in this book may have changed since publication and may no longer be valid. The views expressed in this work are solely those of the author and do not necessarily reflect the views of the publisher, and the publisher hereby disclaims any responsibility for them.

Any people depicted in stock imagery provided by Getty Images are models, and such images are being used for illustrative purposes only.
Certain stock imagery © Getty Images.

All Scripture quotations are taken from The Holy Bible, New International Version®, NIV® Copyright © 1973, 1978, 1984, 2011 by Biblica, Inc.® Used by permission. All rights reserved worldwide.

ISBN: 978-1-6642-3270-9 (sc)
ISBN: 978-1-6642-3269-3 (e)

Print information available on the last page.

WestBow Press rev. date: 08/13/2021

Jeremiah 29:11-13

For I know the plans I have for you, declares the LORD,

Plans to prosper you and not to harm you, plans to give you hope and a future.

Then you will call on me and come and pray to me, and I will listen to you

You will seek me and find me when you seek me with all your heart.

*Grief is real! It is the emotional
cross you bear, after losing someone
you love.*

*Grief does not have a time limit,
but time will heal and lessen the hurt.
It is possible to find a purpose
to live.*

JMS,CGSS

*Grief is hard. It can consume your life
John M Samony Sr, CGSS*

JMS,CGSS

Statistics on grief and loss show that a large part of the U.S Population grieves each year. While some mourn the loss of close friends or relatives, others face the loss of jobs, pets and personal relationships.

Grief is a complex and painful experience unique to each individual, but nearly everyone goes through it.

Grief Prevalence: It is unclear what the exact prevalence of grief is in the U.S. However, these facts and figures shed some light on this relatable experience. Older adults experience grief at a higher rate than younger adults or children. Spousal loss is common in older adults as well as the death of friends, siblings and cousins.

About 2.5 million people die in the United States annually, each leaving an average of five grieving people behind. It's estimated that 1.5 million children (5% of children in the United States) have lost one or both parents by age 15.

The Recovery Village

By Erika Krull, LMHP
Editor Jonathan Strum
Medically Reviewed By Nanci Stockwell, LCSW, MBA

Updated on 11/06/20

CONTENTS

Preface xiii

Prologue xv

PART I: GRIEF IS REAL

CHAPTER ONE
Who Am I? 1

CHAPTER TWO
Introduction 5

CHAPTER THREE
Life Happens 8

CHAPTER FOUR
The Morning After 11

CHAPTER FIVE
Grief 15

CHAPTER SIX
Guilt 28

CHAPTER SEVEN
The Heartache of Loss 32

CHAPTER EIGHT
Loss of a Child 35

PART II: SURVIVING YOUR LOSS

CHAPTER NINE
Personal Struggle 41

CHAPTER TEN
Rituals and Rememberance...44

CHAPTER ELEVEN
A Journey Forword..47

CHAPTER TWELVE
Finding the Future..51

CHAPTER THIRTEEN
Being Alone 53

CHAPTER FOURTEEN
Companionship 59

PART III: STARTING A NEW LIFE

CHAPTER FIFTEEN
A New Love 71

CHAPTER SIXTEEN
Expectations..78

CHAPTER SEVENTEEN
Life Goes On 85

Epilogue...89
Reader's Guide 91
About the Author 93
Acknowledgements...95
Reference 97

PREFACE

When I lost my spouse I spent hours searching the internet and book store trying to find a resource that would help me understand my grief. I tried almost daily but was not able to find what I wanted. I decided that my life had changed and I had to try to understand what that meant.

One day as I was searching the internet, I came across a book, by Dr. Keith Cobb, who wrote *Survival Handbook: A guide from heartache to healing*, "The death of a spouse is rated as one of the most distressing events in life — an event that one spouse in every couple must eventually face. Some people find it helpful to write letters to their lost partner. This can help you sort out your feelings, and still feel connected to the love and life." I followed his advice and started to write a letter. The more I wrote the more I began to realize I may have a basis for a book.

I heard it said if you cannot find what you need; why not write your own, after some soul searching I decided I would try to take on this task. However, I knew there are hundreds of books on grief, death and dying. I wanted to write my own story to share my experiences with others who find themselves unable to accept their loss and understand they have a life to live.

To write this book, I used my own life, interviews with widows and widowers, friends and family who lost a loved one, on line research and attending bereavement sessions. After five years, you are now reading the results of my hard work. I hope you will find this book helpful and a guide that you will share with your friends and family on your journey to a new life.

PROLOGUE

September 23, 2014 was a sunny and crisp fall day. It was the type of day that made you want to spend time outside in a park having a picnic, playing sports or maybe just lying on the grass having a lazy day appreciating the beautiful blue sky and sunshine. The clouds were up high and just rolling across the sky. The slight breeze swayed the branches on a nearby tree. We should have been enjoying the picture perfect day. However, the beauty of that day escaped me. As my mind cleared I wondered why so many people were standing in a circle? Maybe it's a special occasion. No? Not really! Everyone is dressed in their Sunday best. I felt I was outside the circle looking at this gathering. It did not seem right. The attire was not what someone would wear to a park for a relaxing day off. Some people are weeping, they all seemed very sad. What was happening?

I noticed a Priest, standing in the middle of the group. He looked like he was saying prayers. Suddenly I realized this was not a park, but a cemetery. The Priest and all the people were standing at a grave site. Why were we here? What happened to bring all these people to this place on this day? The Priest said a few words as the people passed the grave. They each placed a single rose on the casket. They began to walk away from the gravesite to a line of cars that were parked on the roadway. As the people moved slowly to their cars, an elderly man was seen walking with his head down, shoulders slumped forward. A man and woman seemed to be supporting him. He was slowly making his way to a limousine. As he started to enter the limousine, someone said, "John, are you okay"? He didn't answer. This was a dreadful day. John had just laid his spouse to rest after fifty-four years of marriage. On this fateful day, his journey began…

At that exact moment,
every single thing
about my life
changed.

FOREVER

Michelle Russell

PART I
Grief is Real

*There is no guarantee that
you will see a sunset or sunrise.*

JMS,CGSS

CHAPTER ONE

Who Am I?

I am an eighty year old senior. Since losing my spouse I chose to work part time jobs to fill the days and nights. While making my rounds as a security officer I came by the Chapel about five in the morning. It was still early so the chapel was dark except for a few security night lights that provided a somewhat eerie feel inside the chapel. I started to have an emotional moment so I just sat in a pew and tried to gain my composure. As first light began to shine through the stained glass windows, I knelt down to say a prayer. I wanted to ask God to help me find my way to my new life.

As the morning light beamed through the windows the inside of the Chapel surroundings became brighter. I wondered if this was His way of telling me all is not lost and I will find my way forward. It will take time and energy, but I needed to develop a solution.

Well this book is about my journey forward. Someone came up with the phrase; your life is a gift that we cannot waste? It is a journey. Some of it is good, some bad, some just life. We laugh, we cry, we fret, we worry about family, friends, even ourselves. That's all a part of life, our life's story so to speak.

I am not me!

Why would I even say that? Well think about it, as a couple it was always us or you and I. Now it is I and me.

I am not me. What does that mean? When I spoke to others who have lost a spouse, this seems to be a normal belief. You spend days just going through the motions. You live it but, in the end, you are alone in so many ways. So that is why I say, "I am not me."

How are we supposed to know what is in front of us? Each and every day we wake up to our jobs, family, stress, sadness, and emotional well being, but it's a challenge.

I am sure some emotions cannot be repaired. It's time for me to become me. How can I define that? I actually do not have a clue. My journey is a day by day process. I want closure. Maybe that's called coping but I'm not sure about that. I now realized after a few years I had my own life to evaluate and decide my future. As I write this I cannot say I know what that is just yet but, there is time for me to heal myself. I will reiterate in this book that there is no structured process for grief. It's personal to you. Of course, my family and my friends are the ones I can count on for support. I understand that when one spouse dies, the "couple" is broken into a single person. Now you are a single person and when you are in the presence of couples, you can feel like an outsider because your spouse is not with you. I believe that good friends will try to understand your struggle and are so important for your well being and moving on with your life. Here are my ten most important recommendations that came from this personal experience:

a. Do not hide from reality.
b. Do not ignore your grief, guilt or sadness.
c. Do not ignore what happened. Whether or not the passing of your spouse was sudden or after a long and difficult illness, it doesn't matter. It is a terrible personal loss.
d. Do not blame yourself.
e. Do not ignore the challenge of your journey forward.
f. Do not make any quick decisions.
g. Do seek help from your family and friends. Their support can be amazing for your healing. Find a plan that works for you.
h. Do seek a spiritual blessing for comfort.
i. Do say your loved ones name, and speak often of the memories you had together.
j. Do understand your journey is yours and yours alone to manage.

In this book I speak about love, sadness, grief, guilt, hope and a journey. I wanted to take a moment to express something that I have decided, which is strictly my opinion and my opinion alone. When you begin a new life after the death of a spouse, I think you fall into what I call a "Hidden Grief." I am a Certified Grief Support Specialist, and not a trained psychologist or psychiatrist so; to be sure I found this on a web site called, "Grief Link." An article written by Dr. K.J. Doka, in 1989, identified "hidden grief" as, "We generally expect to recognize the grief of family and friends. However many major losses and the attendant grief, can remain hidden from others or unacknowledged." There is a name to describe this situation – disenfranchised grief. This is defined by Dr. Doka, as "Disenfranchised grief refers to losses that are not openly acknowledged, socially supported, or easily recognized."

The "hidden grief" that I am describing is a grief of the loss of a loved one or a friend. Your grief has been openly acknowledged. I believe that Dr. Doka makes the point that the grief is hidden, perhaps internally, from others, because of a stigma that the loss is not acknowledged or recognized. I do not believe that relates to my personal situation.

Unless the person is screaming, crying, or displaying some other emotional behavior, how would you know that person is suffering? So I am taking the liberty to change this type of grief from hidden grief to "Expressed Grief" which I define as, "a grief that you experience, manage, share and suffer because you cannot accept the loss of your spouse or a loved one." Does that make sense to you? The expressed grief is with me every day, every waking hour. On the outside we look great, inside we suffer every day with the effects of emotional grief. To me I think this explains "expressed grief." On the outside I look like I am getting better, working, living my life daily, but inside the hurt can remain constant. I attended grief sessions and after hearing from other persons who lost a spouse or a loved one, they appear to be carrying this expressed grief for many years.

I wrote this chapter and titled it "Who am I" for a reason. It is the morning after your spouse or loved one was laid to eternal rest. The journey for your new life starts this morning.

Grief is like living two lives.
One is where you pretend that
everything is okay, the other is
where your heart silently screams
in pain.

Simplereminders.com

CHAPTER TWO

Introduction

E very Life has a Story. That story can include joy, sadness, pain and many life altering events. Grief comes into our lives for a number of reasons. We may experience the death of a loved one, divorce, loss of a job, loss of a beloved pet, financial hardship, broken relationship, critical health issue, or a host of other events that impact our lives in many ways. Grief is an emotion that comes to the surface when you have experienced one or more of these events. This book is about losing your spouse and how to be a survivor by building a new life. When I lost my spouse, I was required to cope with the grief of loss, but more importantly I found myself challenged to make a new beginning. Life, after the death of a spouse, can feel like we are in limbo. We should make every effort to decide what a new life will look like. Therapists tell us that the loss of a spouse is the single most tragic event that we will experience in our life time. I believe it's important to note that loss of a child, a divorce, loss of a job or pet can easily be in the top five high stress and emotional experiences.

One thing that is a given, when you lose your spouse or have the unfortunate experience of facing death and dying of a loved one, it is a daily struggle. Death is not if, it is when. Grief comes when a loss occurs, but it is up to us to find a way to cope with our grief and decide our life going forward. I will share my emotional turmoil, grief, guilt and how I found my way. I will explain why. I will tell you about my experience, by journaling, which I kept for one thousand days. It was this documentation that gave me the understanding of how grief had impacted my life. Each day is unpredictable because no life always goes according to plan. Life can be full of surprises, but how is it possible that a single event can change your best laid plans? You now have to face reality when you wake up that first morning after the funeral and suddenly realize you must face the day alone. Each day from this day forward will be an adventure you never asked for because you never knew what life had in store for you. You dread the next minute, hour, day, week, month or years. You never know what those times can bring. Some will cause heartache and others make your life better. While writing this book, Covid-19 caused a worldwide Pandemic. This created an untested area of grief and recovery which I will address in my chapter on Grief.

Surviving your loss and understanding your grief is paramount to finding happiness. You are a survivor. The Cambridge Dictionary defines survivor as, "A person who continues to live, especially after a dangerous event; but a survivor is also a person who continues to live after a close relative or a spouse dies. I don't want to minimize the heartache of the death of parents or children, but this book is about the trauma of losing your love, after a long term relationship with or without marriage. You suddenly find yourself alone to face the world. In a way, I suppose this book will fit anyone who has lost a loved one, from death to divorce, because we go through some of the same trials and tribulations. My experience as a survivor comes from spousal loss. I am a proud survivor.

We talk a lot about survivors as people who have survived serious accidents or diseases. Those are visible signs to others, but spousal grief is usually invisible because we don't wear our hurt like a scar. It is in our heart and mind. Whether the person you loved was sick for many years or died quite suddenly, the heartache can be deep and sometimes impossible to understand. Within this book I will offer several ways to cope with these important issues. What I have learned was this; we all have a life to live and it is our responsibility to live it. The loss of my spouse is a story that I wrote to share my experiences and to help you understand, there is life after your loss. Yes, of course, we are hurting, but I believe our loved ones would not want us to waste our future.

Our life begins from the day we are born until the day we die. It is our story and ours alone. No matter how long we live, we will have many experiences that will impact us in numerous ways. We pray for help, but other than prayer, there is no plan how our life will turn out because we make our own decisions based on our free will. It is our responsibility to live with the decisions we have made as we pass through our lives. We all have our troubles, some worse than others. This book, "The Morning After," is offered as a guide to build a new life. Yes, it is possible!

Your Journey forward starts
with one step at a time.
JMS,CGSS

CHAPTER THREE

Life Happens

"What do you do when your life takes an unexpected turn?" Susan Krauss Whitbourne, PhD wrote that in an April 14, 2015, article published in Psychology Today, "As much as we like to plan for the future, we might not see what's ahead." She went on to say; "unexpected changes can occur that either help or hinder your life goal achievement. Changes in your life plans may also differ, whether you see them as positive or negative. Typically, we regard life changes as positive when they help us get closer to an important goal and as negative when they thwart our progress." I had that sudden and unexpected event in my life that meets her definition. When you lose your spouse, you do not know where to go or how your life will turn out going forward. I suppose that's also true with any loss.

At some point everyone will experience the loss of a spouse, parent, child or sibling during their lifetime. When a loss happens, the grief and pain of losing your loved one and the journey you face after their loss can be a challenge. Is the grief yours or is it for the person you lost? I had to find that answer.

In the first two years I found myself alone and I was still grieving, lost and struggling to find my way. Am I a person of faith? I think so. I am working on building that faith and living with my grief and taking each day as it comes. Perhaps the outcome is out of my hands.

I was angry because I found myself alone. I wanted to seek help to provide some spiritual guidance and find a way forward. It was my job to look for and find an answer. Should I seek spiritual or clinical help for that answer? I wasn't sure, or is this a price we pay for life? No one escapes death. It happens to each and every one of us because you cannot control the events that happen throughout your time on this earth. Oh sure, you go to school, work, marry, change jobs, divorce, find and acquire material things, and so on, but you do not escape your final date with destiny. I guess, I also knew that in some sense of the word, but when it happened to my spouse, I wanted some answers to find a way to understand it all.

I was hurting and trying hard to find something to give me strength. I spent my time searching for and reading bible passages that would offer me consolation through prayer and inspiration.

I am a religious person and a practicing Catholic with a strong belief in God, but I cannot accept the fact that He actually has a date for us to leave this earth. I feel as humans, our behavior and lifestyle can be our own demise. I try to understand why good people and children suffer pain and death, yet some bad people seem to find their way and can move on. Where does God fit in? This has been the most challenging question for me. There is much debate on this subject. I still have questions about how to cope with grief. I am entitled to my own opinion.

You have lost someone you love and your heart is broken. You are searching for answers to find a way to repair that feeling. Author Gary Roe offers in his book, *Heartbroken*, "What do you do with all the pain, confusion and anger? What will life be like? Who are you now? You are not alone, you're not crazy and you will make it through. Whether your loss is recent or occurred many years ago; that lost love remains in your heart." Sure! It is possible you can find another love. You have to move on with your life however that may be. The morning after your loss will be filled with anxiety, pain, and confusion. This is a time when family and friends will be the most important support for you to heal your loss. I was at a very dark time in my life but I was blessed that I have a wonderful family and friends to support me and be at my side.

My journey forward started the morning after my loss. I decided I would share this book as a guide to others who have lost a spouse or a loved one. I hope this will help you realize what life will be like as you move forward.

If you believe there is a time
limit when grieving… then you
do not understand that until
you have lost a spouse or a loved
one.

JMS,CGSS

CHAPTER FOUR

The Morning After

I t is true that not all people believe in God, but I lived my life with faith in my heart and prayed that He will be at my side during good and bad times. It's no surprise that every life has a story. Each day is unpredictable. Life does not always go according to plan and can be full of surprises. You now have to face the loss of your spouse or someone you love when that first morning wakes you and you suddenly realize you are alone and must face the day without him or her. Every day from this day forward will be an adventure. You suddenly realize you have to acknowledge and accept that you lost someone you love.

Earlier in this book, you read of my anger because of losing my spouse so suddenly. I had a hard time acknowledging my loss because we were never able to say our last words to each other. Therefore to accept the death of a spouse is very difficult to write about because you need to acknowledge something you don't want to believe happened. I had a lot of heartache and placed that hurt at the feet of God. At the time I did not see it any other way, but as time passed I called on Him to understand and forgive my feeling that I was blaming Him. As a Catholic I had to find acceptance to begin to heal. Let's discuss acceptance. I recently read an article by J. William Worden, *Grief Counseling and Grief Therapy: A Handbook for the Mental Health Practitioner.* In the article he stated, "The first task, accepting the reality of the loss, involves overcoming the natural denial response and realizing that the person is physically gone." It is possible you will not be able to accept a person cannot come back. The grieving process mentions acceptance as an important step in grief healing. I get it. I realize

I had to conquer this or not be successful in my journey forward. This is akin to an addict trying to quit. Without acceptance of their addiction, they can't move toward healing and sobriety. You can deny grief and guilt, but acknowledgement and acceptance is the emotional fact that can hold you back and stop you from moving forward. Experts tell us that you may experience the five stages of grief after losing a loved one which is true, but somewhat distorted. That's because not everyone goes through each step in the same way. Some survivors say they cannot live without their spouse and die of a "broken heart." I will comment on this phenomenon in another chapter. You have to acknowledge and understand what acceptance really means in the context of death and dying. Do you accept that the person died? Do you accept that the person will not come back? Do you accept why this happened? This is dependent on if the death was sudden or from a long term illness. So where do I fit into this acceptance? As a person who has lost his spouse, the acceptance is about realizing you are now a single and different person.

You cannot make the journey forward until you can acknowledge this loss. As of now I have lived through more than one thousand days. Time is slowly healing me. While attending group grief counseling sessions, I heard from several people that they are well beyond five, ten and even twenty years since the death of their spouse and continue not to accept what happened. Is that possible? There is no perfect answer.

I wanted to write about grief and guilt as a situation that stands in the way of healing because I believe this is an important step in your grief work. This is where I am. I know grief is hard work and therefore, you have to believe the person has died. Everything in my life has changed. This part of grief work stands in the way of surviving my loss. In the book by, Alan D. Wolfelt, Ph.D called *The Wilderness of Grief, Finding your way*, he says, "how do you find your way out of the wilderness of your grief? You do not have to dwell there forever." I think this is correct because I had to find my own way out. Dr. Wolfelt also states, "Your own grief journey will end when you come to resolve or recover from your grief." If he is correct, then you have to resolve the conflict within you that will require acceptance and knowing you have a new life to live.

They say that time can be a healer of many things. I lost my parents and some siblings decades ago. Was I sad at their passing? Of course I was.

But in time I began to accept they were gone. We know that death is a part of life. I have been working very hard on my grief and guilt survival. I'm still on that journey. Why is that? I think it is rooted in the fact that I was struggling with how my life had suddenly changed. I am now single, living in an apartment, working part time jobs and coping with being alone. After fifty years I am now a single man. So be it.

I needed to change my life for the better. I decided to be pro-active, work, volunteer and find ways to keep busy. For me, busy is a good word. I found I was not thinking about my situation when I was occupied with work.

One day when I was driving home from Baltimore, only a few months after the funeral, while I was listening to a radio station hosted by Doctor Laura (Schlessinger) who offers no-nonsense advice infused with a strong sense of ethics, accountability, and personal responsibility. She's been doing it successfully for more than thirty years, reaching millions of listeners weekly. During her broadcast I learned she had recently lost her husband of many years. I thought I could get some ideas about losing a spouse from her as she is a well known professional. Well, the show is not about her, it is about her callers. I still continued to listen just to pass my drive time back home. I was stuck as to where I needed to go to find acceptance, but found no success as to where to start. I hoped to pick up some insight. I was lost, alone and not sure what to do going forward. Dr. Laura was speaking to a caller who was recently divorced and was stuck in a similar place that I was at the moment. Before I continue, I think divorce is, in many ways, a close cousin to losing a spouse or loved one except, in a divorce that other person is still alive and a part of your life, good or bad. When Dr. Laura asked the caller, "Where do you want to be between now and dead" I was shocked at the harsh advice. Those words shook me for all I was worth. I thought she is right. I have to wake up and figure out how to define my life going forward and not waste whatever time I have left on this earth. I believe your spouse would not want you to just give up on a life. I got the message. I felt some weight had been lifted from my shoulders. So, Dr. Laura, point taken!

I had developed an attitude that is somewhat complacent. This is how it is, so I just go with the flow but it was not working for me one hundred percent. Why? My attitude gets in the way. I have to know and understand my perspective. You need to deal with the changes no matter what they are. For me to start my journey it was time to accept what happened. Only I could change my situation. Perhaps that's the answer. Change for change sake. We all agree that change can be a good thing or very painful, but sometimes a necessary evil. It's been done before and I am sure successfully.

You must find the courage to change and ask for spiritual guidance to follow though. You have to find an answer then figure out a solution that will help you find your way. Here are a few clichés that are commonly used that may sum up finding acceptance; when a door closes a window opens, cry me a river, dark before the dawn, easier said than done, follow your heart and so many more. In my opinion the best one is God has a plan. What it is? Please tell me so I can get on with my life.

Grief comes in three stages:
The beginning; the middle;
and the rest of your life.

All-great quotes.com

CHAPTER FIVE

Grief

Grief is hard. It can consume your life. Grief can feel like you are smothering emotionally. Grief can be unrelenting. Grief is, well Grief. I know it does not seem possible, but you now have to move forward.

When you lose someone you love, grief becomes a natural emotion that can hit you hard and impact your life. Grief will affect your everyday living in so many ways. Grief can come from many other sources you cannot simply ignore, because it is an emotional hurt that is in your mind and heart. Your doctor cannot fix the hurt in the same manner that he or she can treat your cold, a broken bone or an illness. Why? They cannot see where you are hurting, they only know what you are willing to tell them is wrong. Of course the doctor or therapist can prescribe a drug to make you feel better, but that is only a temporary fix.

About me: *After I lost my spouse I went to the ER three times because of stress and panic. On my last visit, the ER doctor came to my bedside and said, "This is the third time you've been here in the past few months, what's going on?" I told him about my loss and he realized why I was having the panic attacks. He was a young ER Doctor who said, "I can give you a prescription for a drug that will calm you down and help you cope, but I want you to know that all this will do is shield feelings, not fix them. When you stop taking the drug, you'll have to face your grief again.*

Maybe it's time for you to learn how to cope with your loss and find a way to go forward." Truer words were never spoken. He gave me a prescription telling me "Use it if you need it, but you should make an appointment to see your family doctor." Since I hadn't taken any medication, I was able to drive home in those early morning hours. As I was driving, I decided he was right. I became agitated that this was happening to me. I started to shout at the windshield, began to slap the steering wheel and the tears flowed from my eyes. As my anger began to subside, I knew I had to get on with my life and only I can decide what that life should look like. My point is this, now that the funeral was over and I was alone, I had a life to live. It's considered the morning after. You are about to start a journey to a new life without your loved one. What now? What should my new life look like? I didn't know I only knew I had to find an answer...

On the morning after, I stood looking into a mirror for a long time. I did not see the same person I thought I knew before. What I saw, I didn't like. Who was I? I was numb and everything seemed surreal. All my thoughts were, "Why?" I know in my heart and mind God didn't create this hurt, but I was angry and wanted to blame someone. I was actually paralyzed staring into that mirror. I knew I couldn't grasp the situation because all I had at that moment was bad feelings and thoughts. What should I do?

Grief hit me like a ton of bricks. I was at my wits end trying to cope with my sadness. My emotions were all over the place and causing my anxiety to become an everyday struggle. I went to see my family doctor who said, "Like the ER doctor told you, I can give you a pill that will calm you down and make you feel better, but it cannot fix your pain and suffering from the grief of your loss. Medication is only a quick fix. You'll have to learn how to handle your grief if you want to move forward. Perhaps a therapist may be an option for you." It was amazing that my doctor gave me the same advice as the ER Doctor. WOW! That was eye opening advice. I guess they were both right. I'd like to offer some insight. When we grieve we start to heal. The steps we take are called grief work. Another point I'd like to make is during your grief work, you'll experience events that I call "triggers" which suddenly take you back to the life you had with your spouse. It can be anything from watching a movie, television show, attending a party or any other familiar occurrence. It's like a flashback from your life together but now your spouse is missing and you must face each of these events alone.

Losing someone you love is never easy to accept. My experience is in losing a spouse suddenly. It is a wrenching punch in the gut. I did not have to suffer watching a long illness like others in that position. Their suffering is felt every day for years, while a sudden loss can best be described as an unexpected, emotional, traumatic shock. We know grief is a very personal emotion. I suppose the circumstances of the death will have an impact on how a person grieves. Does the grief hurt in the same way? I have discussed this with numerous survivors who have experienced the loss of their spouse after an extended illness. Their responses have been mixed. Their comments were mostly about the struggle to watch the pain endured by their spouse. It was impossible for me to understand their feelings of relief now that their spouse was finally at peace. The people I spoke with who had lost a loved one from a long term illness mostly seemed to share the same opinion. Obviously, it depends on what the illness was or how long the illness continued. Many times you observe the great toll it takes on the care giver who watches that loved one decline day after day without recovery. If there is one positive in losing a spouse with a long-term illness, it is the fact they had a chance to share and express their love for each other and say a final goodbye. In fact, I have spoken with some widowers and widows who visited their spouse in a nursing home for several years and remained faithful and dedicated to their love and marriage commitment until the spouse passed away. As a thought, the survivor who had been taking care of their sick spouse found their life was in limbo. The effect on the care-giving spouse is hard to endure because they witness the slow and agonizing health decline of their loved one. They realize they are unable to cure them. They have to depend on medicine and prayer.

I know that suffering a terminal illness must be an unbearable burden to carry for both spouses and is devastating when it happens. It's very different when your spouse suddenly collapses. It is difficult to imagine. The shock is unimaginable. There is another point I want to make. We must remember losing someone you love is not solely about an older couple. An accident or terminal illness can occur when you are in the prime of your life. Regardless of the age of the couple the loss will bring many unexpected hardships. No matter what the illness, coping with the grief is a challenge. If you need help I would suggest you immediately seek professional counseling or spiritual therapy to deal with the impending changes to your life. I do believe that survivors have to navigate through the grieving process.

It is so unsettling that the morning after can span days, weeks, months, or maybe years where you wake up every day alone, and it feels like you're in a daze. "When will the hurt end?" Perhaps never, but it will dim over time. What should you do to help? Unless you have the personal experience of losing your spouse, you do not know what the survivor is feeling. A common phrase when you speak with family or friends, "Please call if you need anything." That is all well meaning and is very heartfelt. Everyone wants to be kind, thoughtful and caring. I think family and friends are at a loss for words and offer their condolences in their own way.

The reality is friends and family must get on with their own lives. The truest friends are those that remain in your life willing to help you understand your pain, and share in your journey. Family is a different story. They try hard to support you, but somehow they do not grasp your loss. It is all well and good that they support you, but sometimes you do want to grieve in silence and they should follow your lead. That is putting a lot of responsibility on your family, but it is necessary if they want to help.

As we begin to start anew, we are faced with holidays, family outings, social events and other special days. These are triggers you will have to experience, as each one is critical in the process of grief work and healing. You may feel that you'll never get through the day, but somehow you manage, even if you were just being courteous and going through the motions. As for me, I really don't remember anything I did in the first two years. In my experience there isn't an easy answer. You seem to just go through the motions of living, but every day you get up and put one foot in front of the other and carry on. Your first year is a tough one to handle. The grief overwhelms you. The American Cancer Society writes about grief this way, "Many people think of grief as a single instance or short time of pain or sadness in response to a loss – like the tears you shed at a loved one's funeral, but it can last a long time. Normal grieving allows us to let a loved one go and keep on living in a healthy way. Grieving involves many different emotions, actions, and expressions, all of which help the person come to terms with that loss. Every loss is different." They further write, "Grieving can be very painful, and it's important that those who have suffered a loss be allowed to express their grief. It's also important that they be supported throughout the process. Because each person grieves in their own way, the length and intensity of the emotions people go through varies from person to person." A person may feel better for awhile, only to become sad again. Sometimes, people wonder how long the grieving will last, and when they can expect some relief."

There are several types of grief according to psychiatrists Terry Martin and Dr. Kenneth Doka. I'm only going to address two that I believe are relative to a personal loss and how you cope with the grief that follows. When you experience a traumatic loss in your life, you need to mourn your loss. If you keep that emotion inside of you, then the grief you feel can be a burden on your growth for survival. This grief can impact you in so many ways if you do not try to address it. There are several types of grief which are related to a personal loss. These types of grief may not only come from the death of a loved one. A divorce, loss of a job or other traumatic event can also cause grief. The two types I am identifying are, in my opinion, relative to the loss of a spouse. However, I suppose they can apply to any loss of a loved one...

The Intuitive Griever: The survivor is openly emotional trying to process their grief. The intuitive griever has to let their emotions be exposed to family and friends. Some common emotions include expressing deep and intense feeling, anxiety and other reactions that are important to process their loss. If they do, let them get it out of their system. Go ahead and offer your support when they want to share a memory, encourage them to talk and help them feel it is ok to talk about their struggle.

The Instrumental Griever: The instrumental approach for the survivor is quite different, in that the widow or widower will be more likely to spend time thinking about their loss and what happened. The instrumental griever will find activity like work, volunteering or finding an activity that will ease the pain of their grief. A widow may be more interested in developing BFF's or spending time with friends or family. A widower is more inclined to find work or sports or just spend their time watching TV accepting that's how life will be. These are the problem solvers dealing with personal or private issues as they arise. They will create a plan to help them start their journey because they control their emotions by thinking and doing.

About me: "After I lost my spouse I experienced intuitive grief, which at the time, I did not understand. I was in that dark place for several months when

I decided I needed to take control of my life. To cope with my grief, I decided to sell my house, work five part time jobs to fill my days and nights and join the American Legion as a Chaplain." Eventually, which took almost four years, I became an instrumental griever and was able to build a new life.

I chose to find some way to cope with my grief. You'll find a way to deal with your grief in a way that works for you. It doesn't matter what you choose to do. Don't stay in bed with the covers over your head trying to shut out the feelings. That behavior is destructive because, it will harbor depression and may create a series of medical or health issues. Ask yourself, what will that solve? It cannot bring your loved one back. Nothing will. That was the acceptance part for me. It was reality!

Grief is a funny thing. It comes in many forms. I was fine during the day, but coming home to an empty house was a challenge. A widow I spoke with told me she kept their house after her spouse died because it felt safe to be there, even though she was alone. For me, that was not the case. Being alone at night was the biggest challenge. Not having anyone there all night was unbearable. I needed companionship. I hurt and there was a pain in my heart. It is important to find a BFF or a group that you can join to discuss your feelings and get some support. Much has been said about the stages of grief. It can be comforting to talk to others who have shared and experienced the same loss. I attended many group grief sessions and found survivors turned to spiritual beliefs or clinical counseling to cope with their loss. One thing that's very important is to express your feelings and not judge yourself. Another interesting point about grief is how guilt creeps into the emotion.

I have suffered through denial by trying to ignore what happened. It was only a dream. It was not! You can deny the loss all you want for days, weeks, months and even years but it won't change a thing. This is a normal road to recovery because I believe all stages of grief are considered an important part of the healing process. We can't cubbyhole each of these feelings. They are a part of the whole recovery. One emotion that I found interesting was bargaining and blame. Why do we do that? Maybe we use those emotions to cover our loss. What can you gain by blaming yourself for the loss of your spouse? Blaming or bargaining is just one of those feelings where you think, "it should have been me." We loved our spouse and would not want to see them hurt, so we transfer that feeling to ourselves.

Let's look at the fourth stage called depression. That one caused me a lot of pain because I was trying hard to let go. I made a two step decision. First and foremost; get out of bed every day, get showered, dressed and have breakfast. Watch the news on TV or read your Face book messages to clear your head and then decide the day's events. You can choose working, playing golf, tennis, shopping, visiting, or having lunch with a friend. Decide to do something. Whatever works for you can be the right thing. No one should judge you. You should make your thoughts positive. This will be difficult, but it will get easier. It is one foot in front of the other, but you have to keep moving forward. It doesn't matter what you do, your job is to keep busy.

I did attend several grief sessions to hear how other people define their grief work. It was an education for me. It does not seem to matter if your loss was yesterday or years ago, the pain is still there. The National Institute on Aging said, "If you are grieving, in addition to dealing with feelings of loss, you may also need to put your life back together." That's easier said than done. Some people recover sooner than expected, others could take a very long time. You say this is because you have lived through many hard times and this is just another one of them. It'll be OK. I know the personal struggle I had, so I find it hard to believe you can just pass it off like a job loss, or a money issue. It's not that easy! The loss of your spouse is something that is inside your soul. Your heart is broken. You cry and ask God to help you cope. We can't take grief casually thinking that it too will pass quickly. Yes, it eventually will, you need time to pass before healing. Give yourself as much time as you need. There is no timetable.

Perhaps sometimes, you do fight grief. I do not have an answer to help you understand grief, because it is personal to every one of us. By fighting, I mean a fight for survival. There is no set plan even though therapists tell us not to make any major decisions for at least one year, but that's not always possible. Your own circumstances will dictate what you must do to survive. Survival may include taking a cruise, getting rid of clothes, personal items and sometimes even a change in scenery will help. This may be the best way to create a clean slate for your new life. Grief can be mind boggling and will impact your life if you don't find a way to cope with it.

I would be remiss if I didn't bring up one important point in the grief process. I have heard this and perhaps you have also. A grieving spouse will say, "I can't live without my spouse. My heart is broken being alone after so many years." This is probably not an uncommon feeling you'll have during your grief cycle. I hear that some widows or widowers, very soon after the death of their spouse, die from a broken heart. What does that mean? Is it really possible? I don't think there is any reasonable answer. There is clinical proof that this has happened. There is some theory that it is a phenomenon called "stress cardiomyopathy. According to an article in WebMD this is basically considered a stress induced heart attack.

I can't stress it enough that you make sure you have support during your grief cycle. Seek out family, friends, clergy or therapy to get the help you require. It isn't easy, but the journey is yours. This thing called grief is like having a pain that you cannot define. When you have a physical pain you can visit your Doctor, and fully trust the medical professionals who treat you to make the pain go away. Nothing defines it. You can't express it to anyone or try to explain how you feel or even describe your symptoms. You are expected to be strong enough to cope. You may even hear people say, "I know how you feel or it's been awhile now so get over it and move on with your life." You may want to scream at them. "Unless you have experienced losing your spouse, you have no idea what it's like to be in my shoes." Some days I go underground (when I am having a bad day) and it is impossible to climb out. I found I was the only one who could work through these feelings.

I recently spoke with a widow who told me her husband had passed away ten years ago. She said, "As I was riding in the ambulance, all I could think about was, "what will happen to me?" That stopped me in my tracks because after all these years she was still emotional, but I suspect some of those feelings was concern for her.

Have you ever considered for whom you are grieving? You're thinking, as you just read that line, what is the point? The question is who or what are we grieving about?" We believe we are grieving for the loss of our spouse or someone we love, but in reality, in addition to that loss, we may be grieving for ourselves? Why do I say that? Why does that happen? It could be emotion, stress, blame, or anger over why he/she left me. I guess that's when you may realize it's about you. That's when guilt creeps in.

Can you possibly say something like that without feeling guilty? I think that this also applies to a divorced couple. Are you grieving the loss of your partner or in the case of a divorce the loss of your marriage?

Consider the difference between how grief is relevant in the loss of your spouse versus the loss of your spouse through a divorce. This seems pretty straight forward, but it's more complicated in a comparison.

Let's look at some common points:

- In both situations there is the loss of a spouse.
- A husband and wife, widow or widowers are required to go their separate ways.
- Each survivor is required to start a new life.
- Their future is uncertain.
- Their new life will be an unknown concerning companionship.
- In both cases the spouses will face personal financial matters.
- A survivor will have to decide if remarrying or staying single is the best new life.
- There are children, grand children and perhaps great grand children that are a part of the death of a spouse or the divorce of a couple.

I have identified some common causes of grief by a death or a divorce. Now we can look at the differences:

- If a spouse has died, they cannot come back.
- Seeking companionship is not cheating on the deceased spouse.
- Getting remarried is starting a second love.
- The surviving widow or widower is alone in family matters.
- Children and siblings realize a grandparent has passed away and is no longer a part of their lives.
- In a divorce there are legal issues to consider such as custody, child care, alimony. Both spouses are still a part of their children's lives because of shared custody.
- Divorce is more complicated than death. In a death, financial matters can be settled by a personal will.
- In a divorce, there are court ordered decisions that dictates custody and financial concerns.
- When you divorce there is a possibility of the divorced couple remarrying.

The point of this comparison is that grief is a major part of either loss. In my opinion grief in death is harder to accept, and begin a new life.

We understand grief can be present for many reasons depending on the circumstances. If the divorce was the result of a cheating spouse, the innocent party may be unable to reconcile that heartache and redirect into a new life.

The heartache of losing your spouse through death is a separate issue. You must find a way to move your life forward. You are now alone and facing a journey without a partner. It is possible that once you begin to heal, you will recognize that you are feeling sorry for yourself. That's your "AHA" moment! For almost three years I accepted that my grief was because of the loss of my spouse. I didn't realize part of that grieving was for me as I sat alone at night wondering what to do next. I spoke with a widow who shared the same thought. That's when I realized I was also grieving for myself.

When we suffer from grief, we can also experience moments of intense stress which requires significant management. Whether that treatment comes from professional therapy or self care, it has to be managed. Grief creates frustration, depression, anger, and can cause health issues for anyone who is suffering from the loss of a spouse or a loved one. There are several emotional and physical actions that you can apply to relieve your stress. One activity I learned was controlled breathing. This exercise is to inhale with a deep breath to bring in the good feelings and then exhale and push out the bad feelings. This will help you calm down. Create a plan when the frustration of your loss causes a stressful situation. This plan can be as simple as changing your present activity. Grief is an emotion that is rooted in the fact that you haven't figured out how to cope with this new life.

Therapists call your journey a new normal. I never understood what they meant by that phrase. I am sure they classify a new normal as the life you are now living. You need guidance to help you because you are alone and have suffered a life altering event. It doesn't help in your grief work to spend time worrying about what happened, why it happened or spending so much time thinking about what if I did this or that. The bottom line is that person will not come back and you have to figure out how to live your life and cope with whatever grief feelings you have now. This is when you start to grieve for yourself. Is it possible to survive a new life? You may ask how I can be grieving for myself. Good question. Some widows and widowers find comfort in remaining in their home while others want to start fresh. One day you wake up and find you are alone to face all your decisions and thoughts. Previously, you could discuss a situation with your spouse. It is now yours to face alone. Perhaps the stress or pain comes back as you are starting to heal. Grieving for yourself is a fact that no matter what your history was with your spouse, you may still have a difficult time facing your journey alone.

THE PANDEMIC

As I was writing this chapter the impact of COVID-19 became a pandemic around the world. Why do I want to add it to this chapter, or for that matter to this book? I hope that by the time you are reading this story, the pandemic will have passed and we are all safe. However, there are millions of cases and thousands of deaths in America caused by this virus and that number is steadily climbing. That means the survivors will be facing a different type of grief over the loss of a loved one, friend, co-worker or anyone who was impacted by the virus and has witnessed pain and suffering. It's impossible to even imagine that a healthy person can contract the virus and may, within a short time, pass away.

How do the survivors cope with this loss? The pandemic came upon us without warning and became a firestorm in our lives and health care community. The confusion created by our government and the medical and scientific community was not understood by the average citizen. I am not writing this topic as a political statement because that is not relative to your recovery. This book is about grief and surviving the loss of a loved one. There isn't any question our medical community was not prepared to deal with the size and scope of the virus. The Pandemic caused mass casualties and deaths which became a natural tragedy. This type of grief is known as Collective Grief. That is grief that occurs when a community, society, village or nation experiences extreme change or loss. Many people have lost a loved one to this disease and did not have time to absorb that shock. That is called their primary grief.

Secondary Grief is what happens when a survivor or loved one experiences the loss of companionship, financial security, loneliness, abandonment or other emotional heartaches.

I have not found a proper label for the type of grief we experience during a pandemic, because I don't think this has ever been identified by our clinical and spiritual professionals. It can be identified as one of the eight or nine types of grief. Do they fit considering what has happened?

Here's my view. These deaths were traumatic because our loved ones died, not because of a long terminal illness, an accident, or natural cause, but due to a sudden unexpected event. In a 2020 article in the National Hospice and Palliative Care Organization in their section *Grief Experience*, they describe "Anticipatory Grief as when a person or family is expecting death, it is normal to begin to anticipate how one will react and cope when that person eventually dies." Many family members will try to envision their life without that person and mentally play out possible scenarios, which may include grief reactions and ways they will mourn and adjust after the death. Anticipatory mourning includes feelings of loss, concern for the dying person, balancing conflicting demands and preparing for death. Anticipatory mourning is a natural process that enables the family more time to slowly prepare for the reality of the loss. The problem Covid-19 created was a restricted visitation so the family could not see their loved one or get the chance to tell them goodbye. In this case, the spouse or loved one was not able to reconcile the death or for that matter even accept the loss because the virus shut them out.

I agree Anticipatory Grief or Secondary Grief can be a type of grief these survivors will experience, however I am not sure that it is the proper label. Let me explain; this is very similar to a person driving, when a horrific accident causes their death. There is no way of knowing the accident happened until a police officer shows up at the door and informs you that your spouse or loved one has died in a car accident. It is this sudden death that engulfs you because it was totally unexpected and could not be prevented. It just happened. In my opinion, this type of loss more closely resembles a Covid-19 death.

I have struggled to find a better definition than Anticipatory or Secondary Grief or the many other types of grief defined by clinical professionals. I am just going to label this as "Pandemic Grief" which I define as, "any death that suddenly occurs because of a disease that has reached a pandemic level and cannot be controlled." I am open to a discussion from any clinical professional(s) who reads this book and wants to challenge my definition. Another concern is called Survivor's Guilt which occurs when people who lose families, friends or neighbors in disasters themselves remain untouched.

We all face great losses in our lifetime. It can be a spouse, parent, child, divorce, close friend, a job, or a beloved pet. When you consider that a normal healthy person has tested positive for Covid-19 and dies as a result of this disease, it is unimaginable. We do not expect someone to die from a virus, yet it has been happening every day. How can we face the Pandemic Grief that results from the loss of a loved one? The spread of Covid-19 knows no boundaries. Young or old, healthy or sick, male or female, rich or poor, you cannot escape once you contract the virus. That said, "How can the survivor cope with the grief of their loss?" People were blindsided with traumatic results.

I wanted to add this chapter on Pandemic Grief because it will be years before we know the impact on the survivors. Our Professional Therapists will have their hands full trying to sort out the emotional damage done to so many people. Time will tell!

As I write this section I hope and pray the vaccine that was developed by the scientific community will be a solution to stop the rise in future cases and deaths.

Grief is hard. It's like having a
sliver in your finger; you know it's
there but when you try to pick
up something you can feel the pain.
JMS,CGSS

CHAPTER SIX

Guilt

In the previous chapters I have offered my opinion on how to face your grief. Guilt is usually a part of your healing process. How can that be? I believe guilt is just a totally different phase of your survival. Much has been said about it, but how do you define guilt? What are you guilty of? The dictionary describes guilt as, "a feeling of responsibility or remorse for some offense, crime, wrong, etc., whether real or imagined." In a Psychology Today article written by Susan Krauss Whitbourne she states, "Guilt is for something you did. The most obvious reason to feel guilty is if you actually did something wrong. This type of guilt may involve harm to others, such as causing someone physical or psychological pain.

You may also feel guilty because you violated your own ethical or moral code like cheating, lying or stealing. Guilt is an emotion caused by something you did wrong." She goes on to say, "Guilt also happens when you think you didn't do enough to help someone." That guilt usually starts to surface when you lose your loved one. You try desperately to figure out why you couldn't have prevented their passing, so you now have depression along with a guilty feeling of despair. Psychologists use the term compassion fatigue to capture this feeling of burnout. Adding to the overall emotional drain of the situation is the guilt you overlay on top of the fatigue because you think you should have done more.

This chapter reflects my personal opinion and not a professional, medical or clinical one. When we read the five stages of grief, guilt is not listed, but it stands out like a knife in your heart. Why? It is how you feel.

The agonizing question is; "did I do enough to save her or him?" I recently read a paragraph on guilt published in the "Grief Recovery Handbook" by two authors, John W James and Russell Friedman. These two authors have been working with grievers for more than thirty years. So I'll yield to their vast experience on recovery. They quote the dictionary definition that "guilt implies intent to harm" You had no intent to harm your spouse whether they died suddenly without warning or had experienced a long terminal illness. You may have unfounded guilt feelings because your spouse died and you are still here. What are you guilty of? Nothing! Is guilt just a word we hide behind? I have talked about this to other people who have lost a spouse without getting a real answer. When you have a friend or family member that has experienced the loss of a spouse, they are more likely to understand. You can talk freely to them because they are in the same situation.

I am going to go in another direction than Messers James and Freidman. Our guilt is not guilt in the sense of a dictionary definition, but perhaps a feeling of loss because your spouse is gone and you were powerless to prevent their death. While researching this topic I found this web site, *Belief net* is a leading lifestyle site dedicated to faith and inspiration. "Guilt is one of the most powerful negative reactions to the loss of a loved one, equaled only by anger as a common grief experience." After someone close to us dies, we think back to events, conversations, or modes of behavior we engaged in before the death. We examine the way in which we believe we played a vital role in that person's final decline, accident, or illness. Often, we assume responsibility for their death, which can range from thinking we were unkind or unhelpful to thinking we actually caused the death. We are conditioned to help someone in trouble. If we follow that thinking then how do we understand the dictionary or the definition of James and Friedman? What is the basis for this guilt felt after losing a loved one? I would like to invoke the author, Elisabeth Kubler-Ross who wrote *On Grief and Grieving* about the stages for clarification in grief and loss. The stages have evolved since their introduction and they may have been very misunderstood over the past three decades. In fact in a book by Alan D. Wolfelt PhD who wrote, "The concept of the stages of grief was popularized by Dr. Kubler-Ross in her book on *Death and Dying, but* it was never intended for her stages to be interpreted as a rigid, linear sequence to be followed by mourners." If that is the case then her five stages of grief are intended to relate to me as a mourner. Somehow I found them to be quite relative to my own grief even though they were never meant to help tuck my messy emotions into a neat package. I saw them as a response to loss that many people have, but there is no typical loss. Our grief and our guilt are as individual as our lives. Perhaps the guilt I feel is just that. It is mine and mine alone.

The five stages that Dr. Kubler-Ross quoted are; denial, anger, bargaining, depression and acceptance. These may be a part of the framework that makes up our learning to live with our loss. Perhaps denial is used as a crutch for our grief. How can you deny that your loved one has passed away? You saw them laid to rest and now you miss them. You cannot ignore the facts. Don't use guilt as a crutch to mask your feelings or your life will not go forward. You should accept reality.

I now want to add my thoughts on other stages; unexpected event, reconciliation, journey and separate ways. In my opinion, journey trumps all the others. That is where we acquire the tools to help us identify what we may be feeling, but they are not stops to your grief work. Not everyone goes through all of them or in a prescribed order. Our hope is that with these stages comes the knowledge of grief's terrain, making us better equipped to cope with life and loss. At times, people in grief may often report more stages. Just remember your grief is as unique as you are as a person.

Where does it end? Grief and Guilt are like two weighted burdens you carry on your shoulders and in your head with you every day. It is not like the usual pressures we carry in our day to day living. It is painful in that you know no matter what you do, say, try, believe, your loved one will not be coming back to answer any questions you may still have in your heart and mind. You may just carry them like a load of bricks on your shoulders and need some hope that your guilt is somewhat diminished even if only slightly as you continue your grief work. Perhaps time will be a catalyst to remove these feeling of guilt.

Guilt is an emotional feeling you
have when you lose someone
you love, but Guilt can be a part of
the entire grief process.

JMS,CGSS

CHAPTER SEVEN

The Heartache of Loss

I did a lot of research about the grief we experience on death and dying. What I did learn is that losing your spouse or someone you love was traumatic in so many ways you don't realize it until it actually happens to you. You are not alone in your situation. I spoke with many people on the perspective of their loss. It doesn't seem to matter how or when that person died the heartache is still the same. I think what stands out is, however the loss occurred; there is an emotional grief that's attached to it to identify three stages of loss that will have an impact on your survival.

First is when your spouse or loved one dies suddenly. This was what happened to me. I have heard survivors, which include me, say, "I never got the chance to say goodbye or I never said, "I love you." These words relate to your loss because you think and feel those words are necessary to express your love for that deceased person. All that may be true, because what matters is how you feel about the loss.

Second is when your spouse or love one has a terminal illness or injury and needs constant medical supervision. I say the loss is a loss, no matter how you have to deal with their illness. In this case, the spouse or loved one is alert, talking and expressing their emotions. Your grief starts as you watch that person slip away. If the illness lasted a long time you may feel some relief when they finally are at peace.

Third is when your spouse or loved one has a terminal illness and has reached the point where there isn't any medical hope to save that person. In some cases the family has the loved one come home and be together until God takes them. I worked with a widow who was trying to cope with this situation. Every day for several weeks the loved one continued to be at home lying in a hospital bed with in home nursing care. This widow told me after her loved one was diagnosed a few years ago with cancer, she lived every day with heartache because she had the premonition that he would not survive. It was just a matter of time until she lost her loved one. It was the most excruciating pain to see him every day and not even be able to talk to him. This may be the hardest grief you'll ever experience if that person is your spouse, child or a sibling.

There seems to be a difference of opinion in how the survivor handles the grief of their loss. Some of the survivors told me, "My loved ones suffered a long time wanting this to come to an end." With some of those who were terminally ill, the survivor told me that person seemed to know the end was very near and within a few days that person did pass away. I am offering my opinion on these three stages only, but what I am relating to is from personal experience and talking to other survivors.

For those survivors, they told me they felt comfort to have had the opportunity to be with their spouse to their final day. These survivors expressed what they believed; that it was much harder when the loss is sudden. I experienced that personally but I feel there are differing views on each scenario. When you think about loss, grief and recovery, it is true that coping with a loss from any stage is hard enough. Perhaps, when the loss is sudden, that person is gone and you do not spend those days, weeks, months or years watching the illness ravage their body. You read in my chapter on grief about the sudden passing of a loved one. It is even mentioned in my section on the Pandemic. In a situation where the person is terminal and sent to a home hospice, your grief starts at knowing that person will not recover. The widow who lost her loved one after a home hospice told me that losing someone suddenly allows the survivor to start to heal immediately. In the long term illness stage we experience the Anticipatory Grief of knowing death is not if, it's when.

When we really think about it, perhaps the pain of grief is on both widower and widow due to that long illness. Eventually it is truly a relief because the responsibility to provide medical care and a financial burden the illness may have caused is coming to an end. I can't answer that one. If a loved one is moved to a hospice facility, that is another dynamic to cope with for both patient and survivor. So which is better? There is some thought that when the loved one dies after a long illness, the survivor has already been grieving for months or years. They do not process grief the same as a survivor who lost a spouse suddenly. As I wrote this book I considered this many times. I think in the case of a spouse dying suddenly it is a blessing for the deceased and a hardship for the survivor. When the spouse or loved one dies from a long and difficult illness their passing is more of an end to their pain. The survivor still does experience the hardship of the loss, but their grief continues through the agony of seeing their loved one's life ebb away. Although they are somewhat relived that it is over for their loved one, a new grief starts after their passing. I have to leave that answer to the professional therapists and religious leaders and to each individual survivor.

Perhaps only time will
heal the heartache.
JMS,CGSS

CHAPTER EIGHT
Loss of a Child

D r. Kenneth Doka in his Psychology Today (2017) article dealing with the Death of a Child said, "You never expect to bury your children no matter how old or young they are at the time of death. The death of a child, then, is a deeply complicated loss that challenges parents on so many levels." This may be considered one of the hardest losses we can face in our life. The loss of a child for parents is in its own right a terrible tragedy, but the loss of a sibling is also complicated because it will impact and change the life of the surviving siblings. Whether the child's death occurred as an infant, toddler, teenager or adult, a constant in your life has been shattered.

Throughout this book I have focused on the loss of a spouse as one of the most traumatic events that will change your life forever. That's so true. I did talk briefly about losing a child, parent, sibling, job, pet or going through a divorce. However, after giving this much thought I decided I wanted to add this chapter to address the loss of a child. Losing a child has never happened to me, but I can imagine the grief and emotional despair. My God, that's inconceivable, but it does happen. I previously discussed that every life has a story. This is one part of your life's story. When you lose a child, it is an impossible loss in so many ways to accept.

Dr. Doka continues "It shatters assumptions of what the world should be. It may cause you to question your beliefs as you try to find answers for questions that cannot be answered. A child's death is a family loss. Everyone in the family is affected—fathers, mothers, brothers, sisters, grandparents, aunts, and uncles. This may make it more difficult to get support from those around you as each person copes with their own, deeply personal sense of loss" The loss of a child is something we believe is not supposed to happen. Your grief may follow the usual symptoms but as a parent this is a loss that is hard to justify and accept. I have attended bereavement sessions where I listened to a couple discuss the loss of their pregnant daughter from a vehicle accident. Although it was several years ago, they cannot reconcile their loss, because they not only lost their child, they lost a grandchild. Another couple explained after they lost their child, they chose to travel and took a cruise just to try to cope with the loss. We all grieve differently so who can question whether these parents did the right or wrong thing. It was their choice. Parents mourn the loss of a child regardless of their age, because the emotional impact can be the same. I am sure the Mother who gave birth to the child will feel the loss more.

A Mother and Father do not expect to outlive their children. It seems unnatural to even think that way. The age at the child's death brings different emotions that run from the loss of a young child to an adult. When the child is an adult the loss can be even harder and that loss impacts the entire family. Perhaps as a parent you may feel a failure because you could not save your child.

I was able to speak with a senior widow, Mary (not her real name), who asked me for support after her adult daughter, April, had a cancer relapse. At the hospital the doctors told her there was nothing more they could do for her daughter because the cancer became aggressive and was spreading. It was April's decision to leave the hospital and go home to be with her family which was an emotional situation for the entire family. They were faced with her care with no positive outcome. Essentially, they all began to grieve while they now cared for April through a hospice program.

This was an unusual situation for Mary who lost her spouse and her baby boy when she was just a very young mother. It was more than Mary could bear. Burdened with overwhelming grief, she was forced to accept her daughter's fate, even though she could not accept nor rationalize the possibility of April passing away. I can understand the heartache of watching a loved one suffer with a terminal illness. As the disease continues to slowly take a life, the parents and family are grieving every day that their loved one must endure their illness. Mary asked me to be with her and her family during April's time in hospice. It was the first time I witnessed, up close, the heartache and emotional toll on family members. Their grief did not, in my opinion, follow the typical grief types we find in the loss of a spouse. It was my observation that each family member had to find their own way to cope with their grief. I observed some siblings wanted to deny April's situation of a terminal illness with questions; will she be okay if we pray hard enough?

Weeks passed when Mary called me again to tell me her daughter, April, had passed away. Once again Mary said," how much am I supposed to handle? I faced losing my baby, then my spouse and now my daughter. Why me, I didn't do anything wrong to deserve this?" I explained to Mary that she had no control over the cancer and was powerless to heal April. As I spoke with her the most evident emotional behavior was her grief. For weeks and months Mary was grieving for April. What she did not realize, she was grieving for April but also for herself.

April's husband and her children will be faced with the grief of losing their spouse and mother. His grief will take time to heal as I have written several chapters about grief, guilt and survival. However, the siblings must cope with losing a sister. They are asking, "What Now"?

A few weeks after April passed away, her brother wanted to see me. He was having a tough time coping with her loss and struggled every day with trying to understand why his sister passed away. One point he made was, he lost his younger sister and wasn't sure how to feel about now becoming the big brother, so to speak.

Is it true another sibling would take April's role? Is it Mary's responsibility to step up as the matriarch and be the glue that keeps siblings, aunts, uncles, nephews and grandchildren together? I can't answer that question, however that may be reality in many families who lost a child.

In general, the grief after the loss of a sibling can be complicated because surviving siblings may regret they did not have a better relationship with the deceased. A sibling will think their grief will overshadow the parent's loss of their child over theirs. Perhaps you don't have the right to feel grief in the same way as that of the rest of the family.

I am aware of a situation that when a child dies, the stress on the parents sometimes can cause a break up in the marriage. Why? How each parent grieves coupled with their personal pain may be a catalyst that impacts their capability to cope with the loss. The marriage may be a solid union and both parents will stick together to understand and accept what has happened. However if the marriage relationship had problems, the death of a child could cause the marriage to collapse. I pointed out earlier in this chapter some examples of how parents and siblings have handled their loss. Parents collectively or individually can seek therapists and spiritual help, medical stability through drugs or whatever method best provides the emotional support. I cannot judge what or how parents choose to treat their emotional behavior.

It may be necessary for the family to seek help. The hardest part is how a parent is able to accept and continue their life story without a child in their life. I can't begin to understand how a mother must rationalize her loss, but if the father is present in her life both parents can grieve together and that may help recovery. If the father or mother had lost their spouse, then the survivor is alone to grieve which can be emotionally overwhelming. When a child dies the parents can support each other in their grief cycle.

When a child dies the family
can experience heartache
that may remain for a lifetime.
JMS,CGSS

PART II
Surviving Your Loss

CHAPTER NINE
Personal Struggle

When I went to the funeral home to make final arrangements I could not control my grief. My emotions were all over the place trying to cope with this difficult task. The director was a very kind, caring and understanding person. He took me aside and said, "John, I do this every day and most people who come here are in the same situation as you. They are heartbroken, sad, crying, and emotional when a loved one passes away. But a funeral is for the living, not the deceased. The funeral is held to honor the loved one but mainly to help the mourners and survivors. The service is to help us understand the loved one is no longer with us." Wow! At the time I didn't get it or what he meant by that statement. Actually, I thought he was a little cold to my grief. Now, many years later, I get it. The entire ritual is for the living to realize the deceased will be laid to eternal rest and the living must get on with their lives. This is where reconciliation becomes relevant. We are witnessing the ritual at the cemetery, so now we have to reconcile our loss.

I think we have to consider "closure" as a part of reconciliation. Webster's dictionary defined closure many ways, but this is most relevant; "an often comforting or satisfying sense of finality." It is up to you to find that closure to get you to the next step of reconciliation and have a purpose to go forward. This has been a big challenge for me. I was stuck on this for quite awhile until I began to follow my plan and find my purpose.

To move forward you must accept your loss. When we have open issues, whatever they may be, from an estate plan to simply deciding what to do about your spouse's clothing, it's imperative to resolve those matters.

Too often we find achieving closure over the death of a loved one seems an impossible task. I tried to find a path on what it would take for me to get there. Was it professional counseling? Seeking spiritual help? Selling my house? Keeping busy? Finding a new love and maybe even remarrying? Try to avoid using alcohol or drugs for self-medication?

As I read in Dr. Wolfelt's book, he talks of reconciliation. It is a term he defined as, "more appropriate for what occurs as you work to integrate the new reality of moving forward in life without the physical presence of the person who died." He further states, "Reconciliation brings a renewed sense of energy and confidence, an ability to fully acknowledge the reality of death and a capacity to become re-involved in the activities of living." I think this a powerful statement. When we think about what has happened, we have to resolve our attitude that must include accepting what cannot be changed. Why is it necessary to reconcile our loss? I think we have to reconcile or we are stuck in the past? Think of it this way. When you have a disagreement with family or friends, one party has to be willing to reconcile the disagreement or the relationship is tainted. We all know of family or friend situations where some long time ago disagreement continued on for years because no one was willing to say they were sorry. When that happens we become "stuck." I believe this is the same thing. Even though the death of a loved one is a tremendous loss compared to a family feud, we will not move forward if we haven't reconciled our loss? We have to accept that our spouse or loved one is gone and we are on our own. There are times when I thought my head was in conflict with my heart. We have heard it said, "The heart wants what the heart wants." Yes, that's true, but the head is supposed to provide the balance to guide us on the right path forward. I have begun to reconcile my loss. It's very difficult but necessary.

Your loss created a broken heart. Your mind is telling you to move on. How do you cope with this dilemma? You decide which wins out, heart or head? Not as easy as it seems. I have been trying to reconcile my loss, but sometimes certain "triggers" get in the way. Sometimes it's a memory, a song, a thought, a moment in time where I can remember our time together. How do you find that moment where you can resolve your feelings? Everyone I talked to, who has experienced a similar loss seem to agree that time is the healing medicine. Perhaps they are correct. I need to find closure now. I cannot tell you how much longer I will walk this earth. I am not worrying about that, but I do look forward to the day when I will have reconciled my loss.

According to Dr. Wolfelt, "the unfolding of your journey is not intended to create a return to an old normal, but the discovery of a new normal." I think I have reached that point. I am trying to find my way to a new normal. I am not sure what new normal means, but I am sure it has to do with pain of grief that will ebb away to something until I can achieve my "Aha Moment." You will have days that are both good and bad. Accept that's going to continue to happen. You'll experience those emotions as time passes. That will happen and any professional counselor will tell you that it is OK to relapse a bit. I certainly have experienced that underground feeling many times.

If you are in the same moment, I understand that your journey will be life changing. We are not the same people after the death of our spouse and certainly not what we were a few short years ago. When I think about those many months, I have been through so much. It's not possible for me to be that same person. I am learning though. I am trying to become my own person, as each day passes. I have lots of questions and not many answers. I suppose they may come in time. All I know for sure is that I will find a new life.

We only get one life to live.
It is up to us to find our
peace and happiness.
JMS,CGSS

CHAPTER TEN

Rituals and Rememberance

The years following the loss of someone you love can be filled with emotions that will remind you that the loved one is no longer here. A funeral service is a ritual, as an example. In my opinion, although we believe the funeral is for the deceased, I think it is more for the living. A funeral or burial service is a ritual that is supposed to provide a tribute and also closure that the person has passed and was laid to rest. In short, the funeral is for you to personally experience that your loved one is gone physically from this earth. *"When words are inadequate, have a ritual."* — *Author Unknown.* We ask an important question. In an article, *Why is a Funeral So Important,* by Alan D. Wolfelt, PhD at the Center for Loss, 2016, "Rituals are symbolic activities that help us, together with our families and friends, express our deepest thoughts and feelings about life's most important events." Baptism celebrates the birth of a child and that child's acceptance into the church family. Birthday parties honor the passing of another year in the life of someone we love. Weddings publicly affirm the private love shared by two people." Dr. Wolfelt continues, in part, "The funeral ritual, too, is a public, traditional and symbolic means of expressing our beliefs, thoughts and feelings about the death of someone loved. Rich in history and rife with symbolism, the funeral ceremony helps us acknowledge the reality of the death, gives testimony to the life of the deceased, encourages the expression of grief in a way consistent with the culture's values, provides support to mourners, allows for the embracing of faith and beliefs about life and death, and offers continuity and hope for the living. Unfortunately, our mourning-avoiding culture has to a large extent forgotten these crucial purposes of the meaningful funeral."

If Dr. Wolfelt is correct, then a funeral service is your grief recovery platform; whatever the type of ritual you choose to honor your spouse or loved one. A funeral is something physical that a family decides based on spiritual and traditional values to be a reminder you have to live a new life without that person. But rituals are also reminders. I thought about reminders for awhile and came up with my own definition. A reminder is a "trigger" that brings a memory of your loved one immediately into your mind and heart. An example of that trigger might be something like this. When you see a senior couple walking hand in hand in the mall, the image "triggers" how you used to do the same thing and now all you have left is that memory. In your case, you may be invited to a party or a get together that you feel will be too hard to attend. It certainly was for me the first time, but it is one part of your adjustment process on your new journey. This may be a roller coaster feeling when you least expect it.

I spoke with a widow, who recently lost a loved one. She told me, "I went to a family birthday party and had to leave suddenly because of triggers which I could not control. As I listened to my family having various conversation I thought, how could everyone here be making "small talk" when I am suffering because I lost someone so close? Don't they realize that? They should all be sad. What I didn't realize is "life goes on." After consulting with a therapist about my feelings, he said to me, "that was fine to leave. It will get easier as time passes. Do you realize when you break a leg you could only use that leg for a short time and need to take a rest. You may be able to use it a little more each time as it heals." It's the same with emotions. Take baby steps and eventually you will be able to attend a family affair and not have to "run away."

We know not every person grieves in the same manner, but your grief is a part of the adjustment process. Dr. Alan D. Wolfelt said, "The goal is to get over your grief. We never "get over" our grief but we become reconciled to it." Whatever rituals you follow will most likely be a reminder of your spouse or loved one. You will always have memories of your life together, but the memories should not become a block to hinder your journey.

Time can be a healer, but you
must have patience to cope with
all the grief that you have experienced.

JMS,CGSS

CHAPTER ELEVEN

A Journey Forword

I found this quote from Mauryeen A. O'Brien, O.P., Dominican Sister of hope, who said, "in order to heal after the death of a loved one we must first struggle through a journey of grief. We each find our own way to travel on this journey, but as I mentioned before, the struggle eludes no one." There is no easy way to survive the loss of a spouse or a loved one. As you begin a new life yours may be very different, but you should not avoid the steps necessary to go forward. The path can be a winding road with many twists and turns along the way.

Every journey has a beginning and an end. How that plays out is up to the individual to find their new life? With that said, I guess this is where you start your journey. I decided I had to take steps to change my life or I'd be doomed to spend the rest of my days in bed. When you start a New Year, you hope and pray it will bring an opportunity to move forward to face life as it will be. The realization that your spouse has died and there is no coming back can be a shock to finally grasp the situation. The biggest question or challenge you face is how does the widow or widower begin their new life? It can be a daunting challenge to think about.

1. How do I move on?
2. What shall I do?
3. Can I accept being alone?
4. Where do I go for help?
5. Am I up to the challenge?

These are very real concerns. If you have recently lost a loved one, you may be experiencing the same emotions and questions. Believe me; I had to live through every one of these challenges. At first, you are almost paralyzed to make a decision and afraid to make the wrong one...

I was lost in so many ways. I felt I couldn't find my way by myself. I have the responsibility to pull my life together. I do believe it is so easy to just bury our heads under the covers and forget about living a life. I'm sure your spouse would not want you to do that as a reaction to losing him or her. Remember, it is a tough lesson to learn and understand that no matter what you do, you may be alone. I would recommend you find some support to help you cope. It doesn't matter if it is your family, friends, work, or spiritual help. Seek it and you will find the inspiration to survive. So what in the real world of life is a preparation to understand death? We are human. People get sick, have accidents, and cope with disease. Let me explain. Those things do happen every day in real life. When they happen it's important to seek help.

Your family and friends are a great comfort. They offer support in your journey that helps so very much in your recovery. Your friends will be there but, true friends are always there, no matter what. A true friend is never more distant than a call for help. I said, every life has a story which is filled with joy and sorrow with no inkling of when either one will come into your life. So I believe that your true friends will stick by you as mine have, and I am blessed for it.

Do they truly understand how you feel when you are in pain from your loss? What's it like to be alone after having your spouse for so many years? They will answer "probably not." Until it happens to them, they don't have any clue what it's like. So how much has changed? My feelings in these past years have been almost impossible to explain to them, yet they stick by me.

Family is a different matter. You expect your family to be there for you no matter what. They have their own lives to live. What do you expect of them? They cannot be at your beck and call every minute? It is not possible.

I learned that finding something that is not stressful allows you to place your mind anywhere but on the grief or guilt. An example, in my case, was going fishing with my brother. We spent a few hours on a lake enjoying small talk and catching a few fish. The day was sunny and bright, the lake was calm and helped me to find some peace. Being able to relax is great therapy.

Your journey is not about family and friends. They truly do not understand your situation. I have the greatest sympathy for anyone who loses a spouse, child, parent or siblings, when you lose your spouse you suddenly realize you are alone.

I have discussed this with several other survivors who were in the same situation. Their response seems to be universal. I understand your journey may be a single life. I was doing some research for this book and spoke to people who lost their spouses. The question was, "when did you believe that time has helped you start a new life?" Some of these people were only a few months from their loss, others were three, five, ten and even twenty years since their spouse died. I was interested in speaking with seniors for their opinions because they usually had a long marriage or partnership. I was curious as to those who remained single or remarried after a period of time. It was interesting that these seniors told me, "I still miss my spouse and time has been a kind of a reprieve from the grief." I chose not to discuss this with anyone who had remarried soon after the death of their spouse because, if they had married, then I just assumed they made the choice to be with a partner. By the way, there isn't a reason to judge anyone for this choice because we grieve differently and decide our future as we see fit. They have decided to move on. It is not the same as the personal situation that other widows and widowers are experiencing who continue a journey alone. So there it is, maybe you'll find the same results.

I had prayed to God for an answer. I would ask:

1. Why me? What did I do wrong? I know I am not perfect, but to realize my life and journey will be without someone at my side is something I cannot seem to accept or understand.
2. Why me? I am told you have a plan for me. Please tell me what it is? I am searching for that answer.
3. Why me? When I read the five stages of grief, where are you supposed to start? Just beginning at blame or at grief is more than you can understand.
4. Why me? How do you accept losing your spouse or a loved one? Aren't we supposed to grow old together? Wasn't that the "plan?"

5. Why me? I just don't understand...

What I can do is pray for guidance. Perhaps this is just me trying to understand the hereafter. The five stages of grief were written to help you survive the passing of a loved one. I was reading a paper on grief and found a sentence that said, "If you don't move forward, you will not get to where you want to go." To survive I realized I had to follow that as a rule. Until I read that, I wasn't getting it. Of course, in the five stages, acceptance is a big one. You must realize you cannot bring your loved one back, no matter how hard you pray. It's just not an alternative. That's the part about accepting. You lost your spouse and cannot change it so you must learn to accept it.

This is my point. The loss of your spouse is not the end of your life. You decide what to do, then make it a key part of your new life. Do you do nothing or do you make that decision to start again? It's complicated, but not really.

Finding that new life or the journey forward is a daunting task. You are torn between mourning your loss and trying to decide how to start over. When I think back, now, as I write this, after so much time has passed, I was in a rut and did not realize it. Why is that? It is so easy to just give up and say this is it, my life will be nothing more than sleep, eat, watch TV, and pass time alone. That is without a doubt a terrible waste of a life; your life to be exact.

The road you traveled to get
to where you are today is your
past. It is important you realize
you are facing the crossroad to
your future.

JMS,CGSS

CHAPTER TWELVE
Finding the Future

When I started a new full year I gave a lot of thought about what my life would be like. This is it. Now is the time to get serious and find my way. These are my seven suggestions for you:

1. Continue to work to keep busy every day.
2. Seek whatever spiritual guidance you need to find peace.
3. Cherish family and friends for their continued support.
4. Seek peace. Each day needs to be a blessing.
5. Decide if you want to relocate for a start over.
6. Accept life going forward.
7. Find someone to love or accept a single life.

I have had to live this new life on a day to day basis. The New Year was starting so I went to Church early, dreading to be there by myself. When I went inside the church I was reflecting on my life these past few years. As I was looking up at the large cross hanging from the alter I asked God to tell me his plan so I can live my life. I mentioned I wanted to create a "bucket list" from the movie of the same name with Jack Nicholson and Morgan Freeman. I thought this might be a good idea to place some milestones on my journey. Your bucket list will not be the same as mine. I found writing the list was a challenge, and very interesting. I suggest you make your own list that will fit your new hopes and dreams. I think it is good for the soul after the death of a spouse to find a positive input. Perhaps a "bucket list" can also be your answer. This is what yours and my journey is going to be about. I hope after reading this you will be able to understand the road is not an easy one. Time can heal most everything. Perhaps peace will come in time. Everyone has their own plan, so don't compare yours to others. If this story offered any knowledge to help you understand what your days will be like after losing a loved one; then I hope it is a comfort to you. You are in charge of your own happiness and peace. So be with your family and friends and remember the love and good memories you had together. When you face a new day, whether you remain alone, remarry, or find a companion, you have the right to decide what works for you. Your personal happiness is that which makes you feel good about yourself and the life you chose. It is truly up to you.

Happiness and peace
is a large part of God's plan.
Accept it with an open mind.
JMS,CGSS

CHAPTER THIRTEEN
Being Alone

I'd like to start this chapter with the Serenity Prayer; "God grant me the serenity to accept the things I cannot change, the courage to change the things I can and the wisdom to know the difference." What does this prayer have to do with being alone? Most things are not the same so change is inevitable. You will have to accept these changes and try to adapt. Mostly, you'll have to gain the wisdom to know how the change will impact your life. You must be able to recognize these changes and then be able to decide what can or cannot be remedied. Being with my spouse for over fifty-four years, I think I have experienced every phase and emotion possible. Let's consider this scenario: It's nine PM. You return to your house from work, golf, fishing, dinner or any other event. As you approach your house, the darkness is stark since no one is home waiting for you. You enter what used to be your comforting home, but now it seems unfamiliar as you find the silence to be eerie. You are a bit nervous and anxiety is building inside of you. Your emotions take over and you seem frozen in your tracks. "What is wrong?" Why can't you move? You are standing in the darkness and that's when it really hits you hard. You miss something that is gone forever. Your heart is racing and your breathing is labored. The tears start to flow unexpectedly and you feel the wetness on your cheeks. That's when the sadness and pain of your loss becomes very real. You are alone! This grief is overwhelming to you. It is a strong emotional feeling. You are thinking, if you can just turn on a light, it will be OK. You then flip on the light switch and the light shatters the darkness bringing you back to reality.

If you have been following the chapters in this book, you read about grief work and triggers. What happened here was just a trigger that occurred by remembering a common event you and your spouse shared almost every day. As we begin our grief work we will experience triggers that cause us to remember our spouse or loved one is no longer here.

The funeral is over and your friends and family go on with their lives. Of course they stay in touch, but they also return to their daily lives. You suddenly feel so alone. It's a weird feeling since, for many years your spouse was with you every day. You now look around as you walk from room to room and try to cope with the grief and guilt encompassing your whole being. This, I believe, is your toughest challenge. Now let me digress to mention the holiday season. Is it possible to get through the season being alone? The two big holiday seasons are Thanksgiving and Christmas. They are about good cheer, presents and family. But, make no mistake, if you lost someone you love, especially your spouse, you can be in for a hard time getting through this difficult period. I can tell you, I did not feel like celebrating that first and second year, but I made the best of it for my family. You will miss the familiar things you had with your spouse. It can be an empty chair, or memories of being together that will make you feel your life draining out of you each day.

About me: On my first Christmas alone, I wanted to host a Christmas dinner for my family. I felt I was up to it and made entrees, trimmings and lots of cookies. When my family came to dinner I was removing a chicken dish from the oven. For some reason my bare hand touched the hot pan and I dropped the entire platter to the floor and then a wave of sadness and, yes, nausea hit me hard. I just stood still for a moment, caught my breath and cleaned up. Fortunately I had made other entrées and my family and I sat at the table and enjoyed our meal and time together. My point is you have to let the tears flow, thanking God for holidays past, and a realization that you will create your own holidays in your new life. In time it will get better.

You realize "being alone" is something no one understands until they have lost a spouse. I've spoken with people who have lost loved ones, other than a spouse. They say, "Sure I understand, I'm alone when I travel on the road for business, sometimes a week or more at a time." They don't get it!

When they get home their spouse is there; when they travel they can call home and speak to her or him.

About me: In my career I have spent over thirty years on business travel for a week or more at a time. I sometimes felt alone on the road, especially at night, but I just had to pick up the phone, call home and speak to my wife and kids for comfort. I did not understand what the meaning of being alone meant until she had passed away. When your spouse dies, it is a sobering emotion because it is forever. I don't want to minimize another's loss; however I can only say that I cannot compare this loss to any other life experience. This may sound cruel, but it's reality.

I spoke to a widow who had lost her spouse of forty-eight years. She had a very large family who doted on her constantly. They invited her over for dinner a few times a week, insisted she sleep over on weekends and gave her comfort food and care for months after her loss. Her family asked her to join them on a cruise. Although she was with family members on the cruise she told me, "I would join them for dinner and all I could handle was a few hours and then I had to return to my cabin and cry. I appreciated everything my family did for me, but they just did not understand what it was like to be alone on that cruise. Why? Simple, they had their spouses and children with them. I was like a lone wolf." She told me she was very seldom "alone", because she had loved ones with her constantly, but the emotional toll of being alone without that goodnight or good morning from her spouse was difficult to handle. Her many friends tried to help, but when their visit was over, she was again "alone."

About me: Her story reminded me of my own situation. In my first year I constantly questioned myself. "What will my life be like now?" Who will share my life until I die?" Is there any hope for me?" My son and his family also called me daily to check on me. I told my son being alone was terrible. Sure I visited them for dinner, and my close friends invited me to their family events, but it's not the same being with family and friends without your spouse of so many years. Most of the time, I felt like a fifth wheel. A major factor of my recovery was to find a purpose." It was up to me to get up every day and decide if I wanted to keep the status quo or find a new normal.

This chapter is about survivors who have spent decades married or with a partner they loved, and then suddenly find themselves alone. I do think it is important to understand those survivors who do want to live the rest of their lives alone. That may be a good life for them. However, that choice is not for everyone.

In an article in Psychology Today December 12, 2019, by Bella DePaulo, PhD she writes, "One of the most important determinants of whether time alone is a good experience or a fraught one is whether you choose to be alone. If you are spending time alone because that's what you want, then that will probably be a psychologically healthy experience. If instead you are home alone feeling despondent because you really want to be with other people, that's much more problematic." If you find yourself alone, you may decide you need someone to be at your side. That is also your decision and your choice.

About me: My first two years I was in limbo. I really didn't know how to be alone, nor did I fully understand what my life would be like going forward. I thought burying myself in work and keeping busy was the answer. Hah! That didn't work well. I took on three part time jobs and volunteered with the American Legion and local Fire Company. All that did was keep me busy. I was still sitting at home by myself every night, then going to bed and waking up alone. None of this helped me adapt to my new life.

Think about it, you had someone with you every day. Then one day that person is no longer with you as a partner, lover, confident, care taker, BFF, or a soul mate. You pick the title. This new life is difficult because you can't figure out what you need to do. How do you cope? One thing I knew was I needed a purpose and a focus in my new life.

I'm sure you've had your moments of sadness, worrying about what's next and feeling concern. Friends and family try, but they are clueless. You know the spiel, "Hey we'll have you over for Sunday dinner. You can stop over anytime and so on." They mean well and you appreciate everything they do. The fact is you're still alone and it can be a demoralizing emotion. It is extremely difficult to overcome constantly coming home to an empty house.

I have struggled with this loneliness for five years. Feelings of isolation can be overwhelming. I have had the chance to speak to other survivors who have expressed similar emotions. I felt I had no direction to my life. One thing I did know, I could not go on feeling sorry for myself. It's not a good idea to sit at home wasting your time which does not benefit your journey forward.

Here's a thought. First and foremost, you must have a desire to make changes in your life. Second, decide what those changes will be. Start a journal and ask what do I want? You will have periods of sadness, depression and despair as you start your journal. I suggest that every morning or night, take some time to reflect on your life at this moment in time. Then ask yourself "how do I feel?" and write down that feeling. Be honest with yourself. Try to write ten items that you have been struggling with every day. Start by accepting your loss. It took me three years before I achieved that step. I did my grief work and understood it was up to me to move forward. As you read in an earlier chapter, I heard a broadcast from Dr. Laura on the radio who said, "What do you want to do from now until dead?" Wow! That opened my eyes. I had a life to live and I needed to find a way to live that life. I then went to my journal, and listed about a dozen steps that I had to implement to start over.

Your spouse is gone, now what? I want to add some new real life struggles you'll be facing every day in addition to being alone. I will use my own experience and a few stories I learned from my research. Where can I start? Those days, weeks, months and years have been a challenge to live alone. I can't imagine you will be able to escape some of those critical emotional feelings.

About Me: I realized I was facing a new life. I can't remember some details because days just blended together with no meaning. I broke a rule of not making any major decisions in the first year after a loss; I did it knowing I had to start a new life. During that first year, I chose to sell my house and move to an apartment. I tried to imagine and plan what my life was going to be. Frankly, I didn't have a clue about what to do going forward.

I can still recall the many hours I spent in a book store searching for books on grief, death and dying. I wanted to find something that could serve as a guide to help me understand my new life.

I looked at so many books to find an answer to no avail. Although there were well written books on clinical, spiritual and personal stories, I could not find a solution that fit my emotional belief. I wasn't able to find that answer in a book. I thought, "Well I guess I'll just have to live my new life and see what happens. I can then write a book about my adventures and hope my experiences would help me and also others coping with the loss of a spouse or a loved one.

"And when nobody wakes you up in the morning, and when nobody waits for you at night, and when you can do whatever you want. What do you call it? Freedom or Loneliness?"

Charles Bukowski

CHAPTER FOURTEEN

Companionship

I will tell you a short story about a widower I'll call, Tom. He wakes up and realizes it's the morning after. He is standing in the master bedroom staring at the clothes in the closet they shared for years until Kelly got cancer and passed away in May. He's thinking, "Something doesn't make sense. I feel lost. It's difficult to look at her clothes. Why is this? I know I have to do this but I don't know where to start. I reach in and touch her favorite sweater. I can still smell her perfume. I take it off the hanger and press it to my face. Then the tears start to flow. They come slowly but then it's like a rainstorm. My legs feel like rubber. I'm shaking. What do I do now? I do miss her." It took him a week, but he finally managed to remove her clothing by having a consignment shop come to the house to take the clothes away. He said, "I couldn't stay at the house while they did it. I could not bear to watch what seemed to be a final goodbye."

One of the two biggest challenges you will face is getting rid of personal items. Your next hurdle is deciding if it is possible to find a new love. Let's take a look at what I mean; when you first met and married, you were starting out as a couple. You were about to build a long life relationship. You planned on getting married, raising children, establishing a home and so forth. Now you are a senior, perhaps in your sixties, seventies and yes, eighties. You have children, grand children, and sometimes great grand children. If you do decide to find a companion, it will require blending many different life styles. Maybe you're like the Brady Bunch, or maybe you are just two single people who found each other. There may be physical assets between you that may or may not be shared. You have three major struggles, first: what do you expect in your new life? Second: If you have a plan, how will you carry it out? And third: Do you want to marry or decide to just have a partner. There may be challenges dealing with your children. You say, "No problem, I have worked out all those issues, so we're good to go." Hah! Are you sure?

Here are some common considerations. What about assets? What do you do about daily living expenses? What about your homes? Where do you live? I am sure there are other common considerations, but this chapter is not about them. It is about your personal relationships. There is more to it than you can believe. I know, because I have lived it…

I am a senior and have come to a point in my life where I had to make several decisions because of losing my spouse. As seniors we live in what is known as our golden years. What is that? How can it be golden years when we have found ourselves alone? Wait a minute? You are about to embark on a new phase of your life where you have decided you do not want to be lonely for the golden years, therefore you are seeking a companion. Let me begin by being upfront. You loved your spouse with all of your heart, however your spouse has passed away and cannot come back, but you still have a life to live. It's a shock to accept, but so true.

When you lose someone you love, it creates emotional turmoil. After months or years of being alone, struggling through grief and finding your way forward, the thought of a new love is frightening. I have discussed surviving your loss throughout this book. I'd like to use Tom again to make a point. Here's Tom talking to his best friend Joe.

"After Kelly died, I was at my wits end. I had thoughts of not wanting to live. During those bad days I imagined Kelly telling me, "Don't give up on life." You cannot waste the life you have. I don't want that to happen but I am paralyzed to make decisions especially about finding a companion. I was afraid of love. I know I will never love someone as much as I loved Kelly. I can't imagine my life living with another woman. I'll never find someone like her, so why even try?" Tom's story is real. It is just a way to express my opinion as you face companionship.

I wasn't sure I wanted to write about the topic; Companionship! Why? It can mean different things for different people. After much consideration, I decided this is an important topic on the subject of grief and surviving life going forward. I wanted to include the topic as it relates to your and my journey. The question remains, at my age, do I want to date and maybe remarry? That's a great question!

For a widow or widower the question is "can I ever love someone again?" The answer is yes. In this case, love will be totally different than your first love. How so? This time you bring years of experience to a relationship which you did not have with your first love. Actually this could be your first true love. You may have been married for many years, or newly married. Death knows no age limit. I am sure the length of time you were married and together will have some influence on how you approach companionship. It will be different for both of you. For someone who had not been in the dating game for a long time, you have to decide if you want or need a life with someone again. Not all widows or widowers want to marry; some are only looking for companionship. That is more profound because you will never know who will show up, male or female when you will see a spark, when we least expect it. Am I being too hopeful that time will solve our companionship problems? You are trying hard to make sense of what happened, but your life will never be the same. It doesn't matter if the person was your spouse, partner, significant other or how long you were together. When you lose someone you love any and all plans you made together are suddenly non-existent. You find you are now facing holidays, weddings, birthdays and a host of other events without your spouse or partner. However, every day is a new challenge to face in your new life. What you are hoping for is companionship, love or someone to be with that could be a new second love? By the way, I am not a fan of using the term second love. You should love someone unconditionally for who they are and not a part of the history of your love life.

I don't think it matters how much time passed since the death of your spouse. You will find dating can be a very hard thing to start after so many years of marriage. It is a natural emotion to ask yourself if it is possible to find a second love or start a new love with a companion with whom you want to share your life. You are opening yourself up to another person, knowing that loss is still a possibility. You may feel that you are betraying the memory or cheating on the person you loved. You may feel you are being unfair to the new person because they aren't the person with whom you originally intended to spend your life. All these feelings are normal.

Dating after the death of your spouse is so new; you are not prepared for the emotional rollercoaster. However, it is possible for you to get through it. The first thing that you need to know is we heal in very different ways.

It is important that you do not place a timeline on healing from your grief. In the beginning, you will be consumed with grief, guilt and how to cope. This is a very hard step in your grief work. Time will be a factor to help prepare you for your new life and possibly a new love. When you start to think about dating someone new, it is important to realize there are no set rules. Time has a way of letting you know when you're ready to date. It could be months, or it could be years before you are ready to find someone special to date. I said, grief is personal and it is different for everyone. As a senior finding myself alone for the first time in over fifty years, I found that to be depressing, to say the least. Yet, I did realize I had to keep on living. I would suggest that dating is so personal it may not be a good idea to take advice from a family member or a friend because they do not know how you feel. It is true that they will have an opinion, but you need to consider the advice, trust yourself and make your own decisions. You need to do the "right" thing when it involves dating and I mean make it your choice, not someone who thinks this person will be "good" for you. If you are having mental or physical issues that will impact rational thinking, please seek professional counseling immediately.

As I write this I can absolutely say I do not intend to remarry, but and that's a big but, I have learned to never say never. At this point in time after losing your spouse you realize you don't have anyone to report to, answer to, or ask for approval. Is that a good or bad attitude? As I said before, it is now just I or me, not we or us. Would I date? Not sure because at this age I don't know what that means. Really, how does that work today? If I ask a woman to join me for lunch or dinner; is that date? I do not think so, but it is no more than using the term to explain you are joining someone for a meal or event. I may be wrong using that definition because if you go steady, choose to live together or fall in love, that's different. You then have some commitment to each other. Is it just friends with benefits, hooking up, as the young people call it or is it just togetherness and companionship because you are lonely and you want someone with you? However, this is again a personal decision and you will decide whether it is a good or bad idea. Love can appear when we least expect it, so follow your heart when that happens.

As I have researched this topic, I have spoken with survivors who chose to remain unmarried forever and others who remarried within a year or two after their spouse passed away. Therefore, it is a very personal decision and I cannot statistically offer a reason someone makes that choice. In my opinion I can very easily understand when a survivor is very young, their decision to find a companion and spouse is important because they have a full life ahead of them. As seniors in our sixties, seventies and, eighties, I have to believe a marriage could be for companionship or financial motivation, however I strongly believe it should be for love. Love does and will enter into the relationship. By the way, I do know a widow who is in her nineties and would still like to find a man as a companion. So never give up? As a senior, the loss of a spouse also means a loss of income. A survivor that is faced with a financial hardship perhaps needs the combined income of the couple to make ends meet. The death of a spouse coupled with financial hardship is a formula for extended grief and possibly increasing depression and health issues.

I know some people can fall in love again or find a companionship that works well for their new life. There are lots of reasons why finding that significant other shortly after death or after many years can be a positive thing. Loneliness can be a hardship that is a struggle to face every day. What is the point of living together if you're not married? It's a personal decision because some seniors do live together like a married couple but do not have a legal marriage. Perhaps, this is a big but, because marriage is a serious commitment. If you are together, just for companionship, then your personal finances become an issue. You are splitting the rent and bills. How is the arrangement defined? Is it a relationship of convenience or love? Does the couple sleep together or in different rooms? What about intimacy? Do they have the freedom to date other people? There are many questions that need to be solved before moving in together. Most of the survivors I have spoken with are seniors in their mid to late seventies and eighties. Some have chosen to remain single and live their life the best way they know how. Others chose to remarry. Is either decision wrong? Surly not, as I said, it's a choice.

Here is where I'm at. I will soon be eighty and I know I can't live forever, so can I find someone to love or do I remain single for the rest of my life until I am called to His side. I know death is not if, but when so I can't even take a guess when that will be. My point is what if I did remarry. How long would we be together before sickness or death, takes one or both of us? Remember, when you marry this late in life you have to deal with blended families, financial and other legal matters and a host of personal issues. I will address this in a later Chapter, called, Expectations. It's basically starting over. The point here is you lost your spouse. It would be too hard to cope to lose another person you are in love with. There are expectations that must be dealt with in a new love and relationship. What will that be like in your seventies or eighties? You may not have twenty or thirty years to develop that level of love and relationship.

The years have passed and sometimes I think during this period there were gaps in time where I wasn't sure how to cope. Why is that? After all, time passes whether it's months or years. You can feel the hurt like it was yesterday. I found myself reliving the horrors of what happened. Is this normal? Someone once told me the sudden death of a spouse can create emotional stress in the surviving spouse. Perhaps I have some of that, but I am gradually getting over the stress and emotional turmoil.

I do know I would not want to marry just for companionship. I think about it because the loneliness can upset your well being. I have a wonderful family and great friends that fill my time, yet that's not the same as having a companion, especially someone you deeply love. Therefore, for me, finding a companion remains on the table.

I am going to switch gears and say, now that you have found someone, an important matter that will be on the table for both widow and widower is honesty. What does that mean? I think it is about telling each other about your past and making sure you will be compatible. Is there a criminal background? How about a health background? Financial concerns? What about prior relationships? Now is not a good time to get detailed information on your first date, but these are questions that should be answered. As a former Police Chief, I am well aware of the physical and financial abuse that could occur if you do not make absolutely sure the person you would like to be with is stable, honest, trustworthy, loving and free of any past history that is questionable. Please protect yourself and don't just jump into a relationship that is not healthy.

As you begin to discuss your histories, it may be complicated. You both lost a loved one so you'll have a similar experience that can be discussed. Of course, you should never ever conceal anything that would harm your new relationship. An example of this would be a history of violence, drugs, alcoholism or any other critical emotional, financial or medical problems. There are other considerations that include ongoing contact with former friends or relationships which should be on the table for both widow and widower to know up front. When you start a new companionship, that person has the right to know if you've been hurt or can't get over your lost love or not able to devote your time and effort to make the relationship work equally.

You don't just ignore the feelings you had with your spouse, that's normal. You cannot say to the other person, it's time to get over her or him. It doesn't work that way. When you are dating, you don't just stop loving someone or missing them, but they are gone and will not come back, it is best to figure out a solution immediately. To continue to show pictures, or talk constantly about your spouse is a big mistake. Can we just bury our emotions in a file cabinet? Is this possible and is it normal? As a part of our human conditions, we are not computers nor insensitive to our loss. Developing a new love is far more complex than that.

We are very different people. Why am I saying that? When we lose our spouse there is a tendency to find a companion that will "replace" him or her. Another concern is that your new partner will not be able to accept you if you hold some things in your heart dealing with your loss. There are no comparisons, you are both different and want to be together, so there are many behaviors that can begin to destroy a relationship. You have decided to seek a companion, now it's time to act like you know this can be serious for both widow and widower.

We are not perfect because we have flaws. When we work together on our flaws we have the chance to make the relationship work through problems, concerns and be willing to respect and understand that person's feelings. It is important to be understanding and remember both widow and widower have similar grief over the loss of their loved one. Everyone has a past and you have travelled the road in your past to get to where you are today. All I can offer is remember the past is the past and there it shall stay!

About me: In the first two years after I lost my spouse I had the belief that I'll never find happiness again. I guess I always felt, early on, finding a companion would be disrespectful to my spouse, but she died and I am alone. I thought I have a right to be happy and have peace in my new life. I guess I was frightened to think about dating and finding a new relationship that I could love and live with the rest of my life. One thing I knew for certain was I wanted a person who could love me the same way as I would love her. For me, I did not just want a companion, I wanted love.

As you start your journey to find a companion and become intimate with a new love it isn't a betrayal, it is the desire to be loved and not spend the rest of your life alone. However, to be fair, there are some people who will choose a life being alone and are very happy. As long as you enter into your quest for a companion be honest to yourself and your new partner. That is what will help you find someone and perhaps a new love. You have a past but you also are entitled to a future.

Let go of the past. So why not just get out there and test the water. Find someone to date, be careful you do not immediately begin to think this is a friend with benefits; but be honest and learn about each other before you go headstrong into the relationship. Here's a case in point.

I met a widow, Sally (not her name) a woman in her sixties who lost her husband and she wanted to work with me as a Grief Support Specialist. She was having a hard time getting over her loss and thought it's better to find a BFF than a man to start a new life. She felt a BFF was a safer approach to her new life without her husband. Sally told me, "I believed I did not want to have a serious relationship again, because it is too painful for me to lose another love. She felt, and maybe rightly so, she did not want to care for someone again, because it meant giving up the love she had for her lost love. Anyway, she was asked out to dinner with a former friend named Frank and his wife, a former couple and friends of theirs. After Frank's wife passed away he would call Sally once in awhile just to ask how she was doing. So the invite to a dinner seemed innocent enough to meet and talk about old times, or so she thought. Frank was now single for a few years and tried dating, but did not find someone he would want to be in a long term relationship with. At dinner, Frank was very open and honest in telling Sally about his past, how much he missed his wife and how he wanted to build a new relationship, and maybe love.

However, in conversations he would constantly speak about his wife and how much he missed her, loved her and show her pictures, He told Sally he always thought of her as nice person, good looking but he realized she was still grieving over the loss of her husband. Sally told him she believed she would date if the right person came along, She was not sure she could make any commitment to Frank, because she was conflicted about a love for her deceased husband and felt she was betraying that love. Sally was also concerned that Frank had not completely moved on from the death of his spouse because of his constant conversation involving her. She hoped I could offer some advice and that's positive, but I was concerned if Frank actually has accepted the loss of his wife. Was he still living in the past? I told her you and Frank has not made any commitment to be together, so you can't say too much about his loss. I asked her if she thought he has to decide if he can find her important enough and be able to let go of his past. That's the real concern. I don't think you can ask Frank directly looking for an answer. He still is having a hard time accepting his loss. Of course he's entitled to grieve. If he can't accept this loss, then a relationship will not work out. Sally later told me, "after thinking about what I said and how she felt, she decided that they could be friends, but that is the extent of their relationship. When you start to seek companionship, you'll try to fit it into your first love experience. If you do that you'll be destined for failure in your new relationship.

When we were young and starting out, that first relationship and love is very basic, in that you do not have a history. Starting a relationship as a senior brings a new meaning to dating and finding a companion. Your history could be decades long with your deceased spouse and you have to fit that history into a new love. Widows will talk with their BFF's or other widows and girlfriends about first and second loves. I'm sure they spend a great deal of time comparing the two loves. Men have a hard time talking about personal things, especially about dating. In my opinion they find it uncomfortable to talk about their emotions, feelings and refrain from opening up to other friends or family. Men want to retain the strong male image so they'll keep relationships to themselves. Women like that a man can open up to express and discuss his feelings, but a widower may be stuck in the conflict of still loving his deceased spouse and trying to build a second love. It can be a minefield of emotions for both widower and widow. You have to realize that a first love is an emotional trip that involves physical attraction, intimacy, building a life and more. The second time you have the idea of what you're looking for in a relationship. You are more cautious, testing your feelings for her or him moving slowly to ensure this is what you both want.

Now you have the experience, so you will try to avoid past mistakes and suddenly you'll have a whole list of expectations in this second love. You've lost your spouse and that hurts. But, I believe we have the right to happiness in a new life, a new love and a new beginning. I am saying that you need to start with dating to learn how well you fit together. One thing that'll be certain, you are two different people, you cannot, or should not try to make a carbon copy of your former spouse. You cannot blend the second love into your former spouse in image, likeness and emotions. It requires that both of you keep the relationship moving forward. You share your lives in many ways to build a deep and stronger relationship. Seniors can find a new love and grow and enjoy many years together. I want to point out that whatever you do; your family will become a large part of your new love. Whether you have found someone who is available because of a death or divorce, children will react in a similar way. Children may resent the fact you have chosen to be with someone who is replacing their mother or father. You'll get these questions. "Why can't you just stay single?" "I cannot accept a replacement for Mom/Dad?" "You are ruining our lives?" "Are you getting married, I hope not?" I want to remind you that no one will understand what it's like to suffer the loss of a spouse until it happens to them. After being alone, you'll understand if you choose finding a companion to share your life with will be a blessing.

You cannot find love,
it finds you. After loss,
you can find love.
JMS,CGSS

PART III
Starting a New Life

CHAPTER FIFTEEN

A New Love

I 'd like to start this Chapter with a brief thought. I have come to a point in my life where I have had to make several life altering decisions. As an eighty year old senior, I lived in a different age. What does that mean? I mean we grew up dating and getting married at a young age, no intimacy before marriage, asking a father for permission to marry their daughter, and so on. You have lived with your spouse most of your adult life and face a generation that has new rules and norms about being together, marrying or living together. It could be mind boggling to understand this new concept.

Now that we find ourselves alone after so many years, we must decide if we want to remain alone or find love again. Being alone was not an option for me, but that is something you should decide for yourself. For those of you who have decided to find love again, there are many things to consider. Finally you find someone or they find you and you have decided you want to be with this new person until the end of your life. You did your homework, searched for a new love and love found you. You are starting your journey together. You are about to find out there are many questions on relationship issues. Of course, there is the romance, intimacy, expectations and blending two families. What could be better? Not so fast?

There are a multitude of differences when seniors are starting out again? Does a widow question if it is worth the effort to fall in love again? How about the widower? Is he just looking for someone to share expenses, maybe have a relationship with benefits, or is it enjoying real love the second time around? We have emotional feelings, therefore some of us are not suited to remain alone in our life, although there are thousands who do and are happy and content with their life alone.

I have included the widow and the widower in this new love because it applies to both parties, but there are concerns that a new love relationship will have different meanings to each person. There are many survivors who have lost a spouse, and felt they would never have a second chance at love, but suddenly find they are now in a committed relationship. It is important to note that this second love should not mirror your first love. I will elaborate more about that in the next chapter, Expectations. The topic of love has been written about for many years. The core belief is that love is viewed as an integral part of our lives. As you enter into this new relationship you ask if your heart is big enough to have more than one love. According to therapists that is possible. In my opinion I am not sure that would work well when the widow or widower continues to express their love for the deceased spouse. If there is an ongoing emotional attachment with the deceased and the new love at the same time, I can see this is a conflict just waiting to happen?

We believe that love lasts forever. When we lose our spouse of many years, no matter what the marriage was, it closes the book on that marriage although the love remains in a different way. We feel the hurt, but we still want someone with us to share our life. Do we believe deep love will survive the typical relationship problems? Yes, I think it can. Love is something so special it transcends personal problems, because we are able to talk about our feelings and work out our problems as they arise.

You are standing at the door step of a new relationship. Let me make an observation. Your new relationship is unique to you. Love finds you in many different places. So here it is. Where exactly is that? There are cases where you suddenly can find love with a sibling of a deceased brother or sister, or even their best friend. That relationship may be because of the fact that the survivor is consumed with grief and wants and needs comfort. We have the need for closeness and the desire to be loved again. You may feel you want to reach out to that sibling or a close friend. That may offer you a release from grief that feels comforting. It will have a greater impact when the sibling or friend is a senior and has also lost their spouse. That could be a reason to open the door to share your grief. The widow may be more hesitant to let this happen quickly after her loss, but that doesn't make it wrong. I have stated many times, grief is personal and we are required to deal with it in our own way. If that situation brings happiness to their lives, then how can it be wrong? We can't help ourselves. It is different when the new love is a complete stranger whom you meet, start to date and fall in love. Perhaps the relationship starts out as an innocent hug from a friend for consolation because of his or her loss, but it somehow turns into more than that within a short period of time. The emotional grief of their loss places the survivors into a grief state of loneliness. They need someone to provide physical comfort which creates the need for love. "You're grieving, you're both in vulnerable positions, you're both emotionally open," said Dr. Kenneth Doka, a professor of gerontology at the Graduate School of The College of New Rochelle and the editor of Omega, the leading journal on death and dying. He continued on "As I think about it, I'm probably surprised it doesn't happen more often. While I could not find any data to suggest why or if a more traumatic loss might result in a new relationship between two people close to the deceased, therapists agree that a relationship coming out of any death should be gone into with caution, to avoid a sort of emotional "rebound reaction."

Why does this happen? I think it is a case of knowing a sibling or best friend previously as a couple or as friends makes it easier for either the widow or widower open to seek someone who may be a close copy of the deceased. Surly, when this happens, there will be a judgment by family and friends with a multitude of roadblocks. It will create a mixed bag of "happy for you, or why are you even doing it?" I believe if two people fall in love, it can be a meaningful relationship. In my opinion finding love is personal and emotional. Who are we to judge what two people experience when love is in the air?

The courtship was great. Fun times, intimacy, dinners and being together is something you were missing after your spouse died. It doesn't matter how much time has passed between losing your spouse and finding a new love. We all grieve and live our life differently. So there isn't any defined timeline to fall in love a second time, Sometimes, love finds you when you least expect it. You had your first love but that is now past tense, a new love has found you.

The love you have now should have a place in your heart and soul to bring you happiness. Your new love should not be a competition. You still miss your spouse but you can love a second time. In my opinion I agree with some therapists who state there is a probability you can go from tears for your lost love to happiness in a new relationship. Sometimes there is more to it than just that. It can be an emotional challenge to sort out feelings, grief, guilt and the desire for love! Love allows you to be able to remember the good memories.

I found this opinion of a widow on a site called the Widow's Voice (a blog under Soaring Spirits Int'l.) She writes, "When he came along, and we started dating it was different. I knew things would be different… was I settling? I began to realize the way I loved him this second time was "normal" and that I had to let go of my expectations. How could this love feel the same as my first love? I have a scarred heart. I am in a different place. Love after love will not feel the same. But that doesn't mean it's not love." I was interested in this widow's take on a second love. I was in agreement with her comment, "I had to let go of my expectations." This is a major consideration in a new relationship. I met a widow and widower, a senior couple who started to date and then fell in love. I'll call them Jack and Jill to better explain my point and use these names to protect their identity. They began to date, became more serious and started to realize there were expectations that could or would create a problem in their relationship. Jack told me he did not understand what expectations meant. Jill on the other hand had a lot of questions and expectations she wanted to clear up early on as they were growing together.

The important lesson to be drawn from both widows' moving description is that love can be different; looking for the same love with another partner can be devastating. It is not wrong that your new love is different from your previous one. Realizing the difference in two people enables a new couple not to feel that they are compromising or settling. Despite the fact that her late husband raised the bar very high, she may believe that there is now a different bar. In a sense, the new love brings them back to life by a new intimacy, closeness and building a life together.

Survivors face a challenge of starting out with a new love and not letting go of their love for their deceased spouse. How is it possible to build a solid relationship and a new love when the memory of the deceased spouse hangs in the air? I believe that when you are not able to let go of your deceased spouse, then I am not sure you can build a healthy new life.

I found the discussion about a new love runs the gamut about what they are feeling. A widow will have concerns about reluctance to open up to a new love more so than a widower. Why is that? Widows may feel they are cheating on their deceased spouse. The only comment I can say about cheating is what I learned when I spoke to Jack and Jill about that exact thing. Both were in agreement that when they did get together they did not feel like they were cheating on their deceased spouses. They realized their spouses were in fact gone and could not return to them. Widowers seem to not follow the same pattern as a widow about a new relationship. I spoke to a widower, George, who was more interested in finding a companion and someone to be intimate with and enjoy a mutual caring relationship. It was interesting that some widowers expressed only a desire to find a companion who will cook, clean and provide intimacy. Personally I do not see how any woman would want that without love. One interesting opinion that came out of my research was not shared by all, but most; the decision to marry. That is a major step and it does not matter what the age of the widow or widower is at the time, it's about what you want in this new love life. Two important thoughts were centered on seniors. Both seniors expressed concern for the health of each other and the possibility of death of one of them. I heard this comment several times, "I buried one spouse, I am not sure I can do that again." That is a little harsh, but as a senior, I cannot argue with that thinking. You must face that issue because it is a reality when you are older and starting a new love? This problem looms large as you build your new life. When I spoke with Jill, she had experience being with a partner who was over ten years her senior. When she discussed this with her therapist he asked her, "Would you have given up happiness in your past life if you knew your husband would pass away? Why not take this happiness you have in front of you. Don't be afraid to take the chance." This is so personal and the new couple should solve any apprehensions about health as they decide to take the step to move in together and/or marry.

I would like to add that memories and love for a deceased spouse may be a complicated emotion. If the widow or widower constantly shows pictures and professes how much they are missed, that has to be a red flag. That behavior stands in the way of having this new relationship and love survive. If you meet each other when the loss is very recent, then it may require some time to heal. Can the widow or widower actually say "goodbye" to their past? That's a hard one to answer. If it is possible that the love for a deceased spouse will finally wane, then that spouse can commit their life to a new love. Although you will continue to have good memories and even talk about your marriage, I think that's okay. It should be conversation only. At any rate that is a risky situation, because old feelings may return. The start of a new, loving relationship requires both of you to accept the past "is the past." This is a new start. Once the couple has reconciled that neither spouse can come back, they are more likely to let love take its course and find happiness and peace in the new relationship.

Now that you have considered all my points and some I may have missed, there may be a discussion about getting married. Would getting married be a benefit or a problem? This is a major decision in that as seniors we face a multitude of challenges that did not exist when we met our first love and were just starting out in a life together. As you begin to discuss a marriage, both the widow and widower have to evaluate their own position such as do the benefits outweigh the negatives? What does that mean? What will the price be to marry? Here are a few points to think about: Have you both reached the age where you decide it is not worth the effort, because of finances, children, and physical assets? Is this an adjustment bound by marriage? Are you both comfortable with living together? Is there a lot of "baggage" from that first marriage, good or bad, that creeps into your relationship causing disagreements, fights or even separation? I mentioned my clients, Jack and Jill, who told me early in their new relationship and love that they struggled with these questions and had a difficult time finding a solution. Needless to say it took a lot of understanding, but they were able to find a solution to their past, which was the root of their problems.

For a widow or widower, it is possible that they feel being intimate with a new love will feel different. What comes to mind is: Guilt. How can you feel guilty when you start that new love and become intimate? You are not cheating or being disrespectful to your deceased spouse. I cannot speak for all survivors but this is a topic that you do not share with your children or BFF's? Somehow I don't think that it is a conversation you want to have at any time. This is one of those emotions you have to work out on your own or with your therapist.

I read in a New York Times article by Jane E. Brody, *When a Partner Dies, Grieving the Loss of Sex,* who wrote, "You can honor your past, treasure it, but you do not have to live in your past. It's not an either or situation. You can incorporate your previous life into the life you're moving into. People have an endless capacity to love. When you're missing physical connection with another person, you can make decisions that are not always in your best interest. Intimacy can cloud one's judgment. Maybe you're just missing that. It helps to take that out of the equation and reassess the relationship. This can be a sensitive subject, but it's normal and should be discussed.

Whatever your past love life was it does not matter. This is a new love, and intimacy can be a part of the relationship. You now have the benefit of choosing how this new relationship will evolve. If you have the willingness to let go, you can enjoy a new life that is founded in a caring and satisfying life together. Because you are seniors, love and intimacy is not off the table but now you are able to define what it will look like. As seniors your new love can be exciting and we are entitled to enjoy a healthy life however we choose.

You have finally decided that the time has come to accept and live your new life which requires one hundred percent of your commitment to a second love or you may have chosen to remain single. That is your decision and it is fine. You have the right to choose the life you want. Every life has a story. In this book I have used the term "a second love" which I do not like. Love is very special to each and every one of us, and I believe using that term second love does not truly identify what your new love is about. When you meet someone, after your spouse has died, it isn't about competition, jealousy, cheating, or replacing your spouse. This is a new love so it should be appreciated and never taken for granted. When you let go of your past, you make room for your new love. This makes you happy, fills your life with joy and makes you want to be with him or her every day for the rest of your life. It is not a "second love," it is "a special love." Complicated, yes! But, love is complicated.

> If God gives you a second
> chance at love, it's not
> a chance you should take for
> granted.
>
> *JMS,CGSS*

CHAPTER SIXTEEN

Expectations

This topic is very complicated because we are discussing a human emotion that involves loving another person. First and foremost, there is the guilt we feel when we allow ourselves to be happy again. Although this guilt is unfounded it is nevertheless very traumatic. We must, as survivors, work through this roadblock. It is not cheating and our lost loved ones would not expect us to be unhappy.

We are discussing a widow or widower entering into a committed loving relationship. We have, in previous chapters, discussed companionship, finding a new love, finding a new normal or even spending the rest of your life as a single person. The title of this chapter is expectations for a reason. The widow or widower has now entered into a relationship that will encompass everything from living together to getting engaged and maybe even marrying. That's not all there is. There are many other struggles you will experience as you continue your grief work. Throughout this book I have touched on many examples, from finance to family to your own personal well being. Each and every one of us experiences grief differently as survivors; we all recover in a very personal way.

Why did I give this chapter this particular title? This is about moving forward because you have found a partner, significant other, or a new spouse and need to understand what you are getting into. After all, you have spent decades with your deceased spouse, now you have to start anew. The personal struggles you will experience are something you have never felt before. The basic problem is the emotional hurt, grief, guilt and sadness that will, in a moment's notice overcome you. Many times this happens without any warning. Let me explain.

In an article published by the National Institutes of Health, it stated, "Does everyone feel the same way after a death?" They continued, "Men and women share many of the same feelings when a spouse dies. Both may deal with the pain of loss, and both may worry about the future, but there also can be differences." This is so true. In my conversations with many widows and widowers, who offered their opinions on the loss of a loved one, I was amazed that I could not find a common thread in their grief or how they were coping with their loss. But, what are more interesting are the stories of how they struggled though grief work and their loss.

How can we define the struggle? I have applied this definition; "After the loss of a spouse you are faced with a life you did not ask for, nor expect. We all experience the everyday challenges of living alone. Couples who lived together for many years are like one person. That union is shattered when one dies. It is like you have lost half of yourself. Therefore, it is understandable that you will have trouble finding out who you are? You have managed to cope with the loneliness after your spouse's death but that was to get through the grief, sadness and despair. You are starting on a journey to a new life without any idea what that means. That is the struggle I am writing about!"

I suppose there are many common issues that must be addressed by anyone who has lost their spouse or a loved one. I hesitate to make a list because these issues are personal and unique to you. However, I am just bringing these up as they fall into the category of the morning after.

You cannot ignore them, deny them, forget them, or try to tell yourself they are not real. That is not being realistic. I know!

About me: I have lived through all of them for five years and wonder today how I have managed to handle all of the struggles. I sold my home, lived in an apartment, bought a house to start fresh. I did it all on my own. I had my own reservations about doing the right thing. In the end it was all up to me, either good or bad. As I look back on the choices I made, I did survive the struggles and actually did launch a new beginning and a new life.

When you enter into a committed relationship, after the death of your spouse, this new love brings with it a lot of conflicting feelings, emotions and yes, baggage. This must be addressed to ensure the relationship is solid and will survive the test of time. We start out remembering our first love and expect to get a redo. That is not possible! Here's the big surprise. Your second love may not even resemble your first love and certainly you should not have the same expectations you had when you met and married your first love. When you started out, it was just the two of you. So many years ago, when you and your spouse were young, you had hopes and dreams of love, marriage, children, family, home and more. You said your wedding vows, "'till death do us part," but that was, hopefully, decades in the future. It was decades in the future, so it was not something you and your spouse dwelled upon, not even for a minute.

Well, in the blink of an eye, time passed and those years turned into decades. You were a couple for forty or fifty or maybe even sixty years, and then a part of your life came crashing down because your spouse passed away. You woke up one day and suddenly found yourself alone. In my previous chapters I discussed a new normal, a new life, the journey forward and companionship. You have already survived these stages of your new life and now found someone to love. Starting out new together will be exciting! Then without any warning emotional issues creep in and can put huge unexpected trouble on the horizon.

You and your partner are starting out in a loving relationship hopefully on the road to happiness. During my research I found new couples had expectations that needed to be worked out. I did learn that widows were more open to discuss what they hoped for in a new love. Widowers were more direct and offered that, many times, they simply did not understand what their new love really expected. A relationship is not just about being intimate. It is about much more than that. One thing for sure is if you can't work out the expectations, the relationship is most likely doomed from the start. So I am sharing all the information from my discussions and added my own thoughts. There are other expectations I may have failed to include as they did not seem to relate to me. After reading my book, I invite you to make a list of your own. Let the past be the past. Don't let it become a part of your new life. I have placed this as number one for a reason. Therapists talk about loving two people at the same time, your deceased spouse and your new love.

I think a widow may see this as the widower wanting to continue to bring his deceased spouse into his new life. A widow has an emotional feeling that she is second to the deceased wife, as a competition or even a replacement. Wow! That's a disaster just waiting to happen. I think whether the spouse recently passed or it has been years, it does not matter because it is real in every sense of the word. A second love doesn't mean second place. You are not the same couple. The time between your loss and finding a new love plays an important role. You may have been single for some time with no one to report to, as free as a bird, and then suddenly find yourself caring about the other person's feelings. You are conflicted. Your life style is changing. Both of you are bringing important parts of your life and much more into your relationship. It's a new world for you again. You are no longer I or me, you have become we and us. It is possible you will experience some issues with intimacy. It may be that your new love did not experience the death of a spouse or partner, but they are single because of a broken relationship such as a divorce or perhaps a life as a single person. This scenario may bring a different set of problems. You have to work at love if you want to find happiness and enjoy your life together.

You may look at your new companion, with some apprehension, and may have misgivings on many levels. For instance; you must consider, who is this new man or woman; what about your children's feelings about bringing a new person into their lives? It is a touchy situation and must be handled with care. On the other hand, what if there were several years between the widow and widower finding this new love? I imagine for some, they have answered the "how soon" question, because they are together and are looking for a long term relationship. It is important that the couple examine what is it they looking for in this new phase of their lives. Is it a deep love or a companionship? Will it be marriage vows to make it official? Those are questions that must be answered. Seniors carry a burden of several issues that should be placed under the heading of expectations. Not only is finding the answers to what your expectations are in this union, you must take into consideration the quirks of living together compared to what you have been accustomed to in your past life. There are common things like, meals, sleeping, health and a host of other behavioral patterns that must be considered. If you were alone for several years, you were free to do whatever you wanted because you did not have to answer to anyone. Now you have another person at your side that may have different ideas about your togetherness. No matter what your situation was before, you have to find a solution that works for both of you. For example, when do you take off your wedding ring? How many photos of your spouse should you display in your shared home? You should discuss displaying keepsakes from your former life. I am sure there is a multitude of these concerns that must be dealt with together, when it involves your deceased spouse's memory.

You need to be very conscious of showing affection when you are in the presence of family and friends. Remember they are all used to you being with your spouse. You need to be very respectful of showing affection when you are in public. The matter of showing affection around your family can be a touchy subject. Perhaps the children are still grieving the loss of their Mom or Dad and repel at seeing their parent cuddling or showing affection with another man or woman. Children cannot always accept your new love, so I recommend caution and common sense when you join family or friends at a social get-together. Be discreet, but no one has the right to tell you how to live your life. Actually, I have found, until the loss happens to them, they do not understand this type of grief and loneliness. You cannot regret what you are doing as long as you feel and know it is what you need and want in your life.

A separate issue or expectation that seniors face is health and age related medical problems. For example let's look at age. A couple in their sixties can look forward to twenty or more years of life. As the years move into the seventies and eighties, the potential of having ten or more years together may not be a reality. What about the possibility of a widow finding an older man or vice versa for that matter? In that scenario, what if that person is several years his or her senior. I had a discussion with a widow who told me she met a man who she thought was her age. I asked her to explain the situation. She told me, "he appeared to be more my age because he was healthy, vibrant and outgoing. After being together and getting closer, we finally discussed age and I found out he was much older. It frightened me to think I could lose someone again but I cared too much for him by that time. I decided I would leave it up to fate or a higher power." This may not be a problem for some, but it should be considered and the pros and cons need to be evaluated by both parties. On the other hand, what if in the relationship one person is a lot younger? We can talk about when the widow is labeled a "cougar" as they are known to be called.

If we are talking about several years younger, that can pose a whole new set of concerns. How young is young? The age gap could be years or a generation which is a completely separate issue.

There are many books written about someone being with a younger male or female. How can we judge that union as incorrect? In my opinion you cannot. When we discuss older or younger companions, there are always exceptions. If the person is older than their partner, then we have all the history of their life that will come into play and must be reconciled to make the relationship work. A younger person doesn't necessarily bring the same concerns to the table, but those are issues that most likely can be worked out.

Now let's talk about compatibility. For instance, say the widow (widower) is in their seventies or older and the new partner is between mid-fifties to mid-sixties or younger as a comparison. They may be decades apart in music, attitudes, social wants, financial security, commitment, even health. A critical point is when there are valuable assets. Is the younger person seeking marriage, or are they just, hoping for a payout that's a part of the will? Could this mean a legal battle over the estate being left to the new partner or living children? It can get messy. However, if this can be agreed upon then both partners can enjoy a happy life. I cannot take a side one way or the other. I will leave this decision up to you. Getting to know each other and settling those concerns are important. Perhaps a pre-nup may be appropriate. It will make your relationship more loving, satisfying and bring the happiness you are hoping for in your new life.

About me: I was alone for many years and was beginning to accept that would be my life going forward. One of the problems I faced was my own emotional feeling of making a commitment to find someone to love. I did not realize that you don't find love, it finds you. I have a theory that if you found your soul mate, partner, spouse, or significant other, you cannot go back to dating. I hope you did date and got to know each other in the beginning. Many expectations that arise when you fall in love are usually settled during a dating cycle. Now is not the time to decide if your relationship is right for both of you because you are past that point. You cannot bury memories, but they should not be a topic of constant conversation with your new partner. It should be a love that is more meaningful because you have life experience and know how to appreciate someone. You can and are expected to make new memories, and share your life. If you are in your seventies or eighties, try to understand and make your years together be a special and loving time of your life.

When I first met you I
thought you were perfect.
then I knew you were not
perfect, and I loved you
more...

JMS,CGSS

CHAPTER SEVENTEEN
Life Goes On

I n a way this chapter could have been titled "Conclusion," but I thought this title was more appropriate. We have reached the point where we must answer these questions, "What's next?" and "What do I do now?" I can't write a conclusion because in every case our life must go on. As you might guess, my story, suggestions and experiences are not right for everyone because you choose how to live your life after the loss of a loved one as a single person or finding a new love. It is your life and your choice. It is possible that my recommendations may not be for you, and that's OK. You decide.

Each year we are all start with a clean slate. Whatever New Year you are starting since your loss, becomes a new adventure. It's time for you to make some resolutions and stick with them to support your journey forward. I have it down to three main resolutions.

- Number One: Develop a plan to guide you on your journey.
- Number Two: Build new memories and a new life that offers happiness and peace.
- Number Three: Find someone you can love or live your new life as a single person.

Here are my suggestions. Take a moment to write out your resolutions. It doesn't matter if you have one or dozens. The main point to consider is to carry them out. Most of us, after January, tend to forget or ignore what we wrote. However as a survivor, this is a very important step in your journey.

As I mentioned in an earlier chapter, I took the time to create a journal on how my life changed for over many years. I had created a bucket list after a movie of that same name. I did that by listing whatever I thought I would like to do before my time on this earth runs out. By the way, I actually kept it to ten so I was pretty certain I could achieve them. When I was researching and interviewing other survivors who had lost a loved one, the number one concern was; "How long will this continue to hurt?"

Healing is a process that happens when you allow yourself to feel the pain of your loss. So there is no real answer, but time and acceptance of your loss can be the healing factor we all need. Let me talk then about closure. The dictionary has several different meanings to the word closure, but I liked this one. Closure is defined as, "an often comforting or satisfying sense of finality for victims needing closure." Although the reference is victims then, in a sense I am a victim, but also a survivor because of my journey. I wrote on how my life changed daily on my way forward. Now I think it's time to bring an end to my story that I had to endure as each day ended and a new one began. Life is a story and it can change in the blink of an eye. I had to live through my grief no matter how hard some days were yet I managed to cope with my loss. I realized I am responsible for what happens next.

After all these years of managing my journey I began to understand I didn't expect my life to be so different. All I saw before me were negative thoughts and feelings. Everyone knows our time on earth is limited. All you can hope for is a good and happy life for however long that will last. I am willing to keep those old memories and start a new beginning. Memories I make from now on will just be mine.

I started my journey with an optimism that I can focus on my life forward and realized it could be whatever I wanted it to be because I am the one in control. You are the only one who will know what it's like to move forward and gain some insight into what you can expect. Each and every one of us must face these obstacles after the death of a loved one. For me the first step was to start to get through my grief, then begin a healing process. As I progressed it became reconciliation and acceptance then understanding that her death was an unexpected event that I did not have any control over, no matter what I did.

Your journey may be quite different. I spent many years searching for information that would provide a real world experience of what to expect. I couldn't find a guide that I believed was a help to recovery. Clinical and spiritual books and teachings were not very helpful because they were instructional and did not provide what I was looking for on how to deal with my life and the pain of my loss. By the way, when you visit any major book store there will be shelves full of books on grief, death and dying. I needed something that would reference real experience to help understand what I would have to go through every day. I previously mentioned that Dr. Cobb suggested that you can write a letter to express what you did not get the chance to tell your spouse. I suggest you take a pen and paper and write whatever you did not get the chance to say. As you intend to move your journey forward, I hope I have provided some insights to the challenges you'll face as you develop a new normal. It was absolutely disheartening to learn not everyone can process their loss successfully. I imagine some people simply "give up" and turn themselves inward with so much grief or guilt, they lose sight of the fact that they have a life to live.

Here are the two most important things I learned. First is to find reconciliation for your loss and second is to find a purpose in your life. I believe without these two important parts of your journey, you'll have trouble being successful living your new life. If I can offer you one more important piece of advice that I did learn, time is your savior. President John F. Kennedy's mother, Rose, said, "it has been said that time heals all wounds. I do not agree. The wounds remain. In time protecting our insanity, the wound is covered with scars. When the wound is deep, time can be a healer but sometimes that wound(s) will leave a scar and the pain lessens. But it is never gone."

You can make a resolution to get through each day because you are a person who has suffered a loss, but you have a life that is your responsibility to live and seek happiness. Remember you do have your life. Don't waste it by not living it to the best of your ability. My only hope is that I can obtain the peace and happiness I am praying for and let my life take its course. Maybe, just maybe in God's plan I will meet someone to love. Who knows?

An important part of my plan in this new life is to make new memories to help me stay on track. It's a lesson that life does move on. It is just one more step in my journey that helps me understand I have to live my life. So here it is. It is time for me to move ahead and accept what my life will be but I want a change. I put my trust in my God asking him to help me find my way. You can decide which road your journey will take you spiritually, mentally or physically. You may go it alone or be with someone who will share your trip, as a companion or perhaps a new spouse. There is no right or wrong answer.

We all experience a part of life that includes losing a loved one whether it is due to health, accident or some other means. You realize there isn't any way you can look into the future to see how it will eventually turn out. No sir, that's not in the playbook. We can ask, why not? Every second of life adds to our story, good or bad. Perhaps it's best we cannot see into the future, because we may not like what we see. Whatever it is, I doubt you can change history or how your life will play out.

As you go forward may God be at your side as you find your way to that new journey. Remember change is a part of life. You and you alone have the responsibility to live every day going forward. I wish you success in finding your happiness and peace. I recently thought about where I am going from here. We only have one life to live so we should not waste it. After some reflection, I thought, what is it I want? In the story of our lives there are mysteries that have no specific answers, even though you keep asking for that single answer to make sense of the loss you suffered. I know there will be an unexpected event, but I have to know who I was then and who I will be as I realize I must now go my "separate way." Perhaps I will continue to search for an answer to share with you in the future.

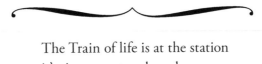

The Train of life is at the station
it's time to get on board…

JMS,CGSS

EPILOGUE

The years have passed, seven to be exact, so I decided that this epilogue was a good place to tell you how I have survived these years and what my life is like now. Every chapter I wrote in this book is true because I lived with the grief, guilt, and being alone every day. I wanted to share my story to let you all know that your grief can be overwhelming and your journey hard, but you can be a survivor and create a new life.

I used the caption "about me" in various chapters to tell you what my life is like after six years. I thought it was time to add some personal information that I will again still call "about me." As I write this epilogue I wanted to add this as a real life personal story. This book was a labor of love, heartache and challenge. Perhaps in your new life, you will experience the same journey that could become a never ending story.

About me: I had not attended a bereavement meeting for a few years. One day I read my church bulletin that posted a meeting was being held at a local church. Since I had recently moved back to my hometown area I thought a refresher could be beneficial as I am now in my sixth year. I procrastinated telling myself I am doing ok so why attend a grief discussion. I certainly didn't want to open any old emotional feelings.

I decided to attend the session. When I arrived, about a dozen people were already sitting at a conference table. There was only one available chair next to a woman. The narrator invited me to join the group telling me it was open seating. I took that seat and little did I know something was happening to me. I previously wrote that you cannot find love, it will find you. When I took that seat next to her, she told me her name. I realized I wanted to get to know her. She had lost a husband and a partner and was hurting trying to get her life together. As the session ended, I spoke with her to offer my friendship to help her cope with her loss. I walked her to her car because I wanted to be a gentleman. As we approached her car, she said, thank you, and walked alone to get in and drive away. I thought, Well she is still hurting and afraid of accepting friendship from a stranger. After a few more meetings, we broke the ice. That meeting led to a lunch to talk about our losses. In my case it had been six years, in her case is was many years since losing her husband, but only months after losing her partner.

At our lunch we seemed to find many common interests and feelings so I decided to invite her to dinner. I offered to take her and she accepted. At dinner, we talked, held hands to support each other's losses, and a love story was beginning to grow. It is now one year later. We are a couple and lived through expectations, personal and family relationships, the Pandemic and everything in between. The end of this story goes like this, I sold my house and we now live together. She is now my fiancée, but we have not set a date. As seniors we are not sure if marriage is necessary because we are in our eighties. We love each other and hope we'll spend whatever time we have left on this earth together. As I end this "about me" I can tell you I have found the peace and happiness I was seeking for six years.

The Chapters titled Being Alone, Companionship and Expectations were written to share these critical steps in my and your journey. I wanted one person I could love and that one person to love me back. I found that person and fell in love. It was a moment in time that I chose to go to that bereavement session. It was meant to be. I believe God sent me so love could find me!

When we have found a
new love in our life, cherish
it, nurture it and you will find
it is possible to love again.
JMS,CGSS

Authors note: This book is the result of countless hours of research and soul searching to find answers on grief, death and dying. I apologize if I have made any references or omission errors, or offended any reader. It was unintentional.

READER'S GUIDE

Thank you buying and reading this book. You have had the opportunity to read each chapter and reflect on my experiences and the importance of grief work. I have listed ten key recommended homework assignments that will be helpful on your journey forward.

1. Keep a daily journal.
2. Write a letter to your spouse or loved one telling them whatever you wanted to say but did not get that chance.
3. If you're able, then write a second letter answering your letter, but responding as if he or she were writing it back.
4. Take a clean sheet of paper and write answers to these words. Your answers should be how you are feeling at that moment: Anger, Missing You, Sadness, Loneliness, Acknowledgement, Reconciliation, and Despair, What should I do now?
5. Attend bereavement sessions to learn you are not alone.
6. It is very important to keep up with your health.
7. Create a bucket list.
8. Examine how you have progressed since your loss.
9. Find a way to keep busy and occupy your time. It may be difficult, at first, but an important step in your journey.
10. Decide if you need a BFF, a companion, job, relocation or something you would like to do. Plan to change your life.

ABOUT THE AUTHOR

John M Samony Sr is a US Army Vietnam Veteran, former Police Chief and Public Safety Director, Security and Business Consultant, substitute teacher and a former Chaplain and current member of the American Legion. His career also includes positions as Executive Senior Manager in industry. John has written and published numerous trade journal articles on business management, police operations and is a frequent speaker at business and security seminars.

He is a Pop to five grandchildren and Dad to two children. His favorite pass time is cooking and writing and is an avid researcher on WWII history. John is a graduate of Temple University with a BA in Political Science and Pasadena City College with an AA in Police Administration and the University of Wisconsin as a Certified Grief Support Specialist.

The Author focuses on counseling people who have suffered from a major loss, whether the result of a death, divorce or any personal traumatic event.

He resides in Dupont, Pennsylvania. "The Morning After" is his first non-fiction novel. To contact John, visit his web site at www. JohnMSamonySr.com.

ACKNOWLEDGEMENTS

I want to acknowledge my son John, his wife Sherie, my family and so many friends that stood by my side as I traveled these years writing this book.

To Joan Lokuta, my fiancée, confidant, contributor, and supporter as we shared many grief stories. Her hard work as my editor and her encouragement for me to write this book was amazing.

To my friend and fellow veteran Charles Burckhardt, M.A, M.Ed a professional Clinical Counselor who offered his advice and review of this book.

To my faith in God where I was able to seek the spiritual comfort I needed so desperately in those early days.

REFERENCE

As a practicing clinician I am used to the sterile atmosphere of the therapy room, and never seem to have the time to get the full flavor of the long term relationship and the crushing blow dealt when one of the partners dies. This book, The Morning After, allows us to see this through the lens of the surviving spouse.

The Author has unselfishly opened his heart to us, and we follow him as he travels through a life after the loss of his spouse. This, in reality, has given us a road map for dealing with grief and a valuable resource for clinicians working with survivors of death.

Charles Burckhardt, M.A., M.ED

When you lose your spouse your life will never be the same.
"The Morning After" will be filled with heartache,
depression, despair and sadness.
As you travel through weeks, months or years
you will start to realize there is hope.

When you process your grief and journey forward, the
road taken will be yours and yours alone.

There is a new life on the horizon that will
finally offer you happiness and peace.
JMS,CGSS

04090024-0083618

Printed in the United States
by Baker & Taylor Publisher Services